THE OCCULT SIGNIFICANCE
OF FORGIVENESS

The Occult Significance of Forgiveness

Sergei O. Prokofieff

TEMPLE LODGE
London

Translated from the Russian by Simon Blaxland de Lange

Temple Lodge Publishing
51 Queen Caroline Street
London W6 9QL

First English edition 1991
Second edition 1992
Third edition 1995

Originally published in German under the title *Die okkulte Bedeutung des Verzeihens*
by Verlag Freies Geistesleben in 1991

A catalogue record for this book is available from the British Library

ISBN 0 904693 71 6

Typeset by DP Photosetting, Aylesbury, Bucks
Printed in Great Britain by
The Cromwell Press Limited,
Broughton Gifford, Melksham, Wiltshire

*Dedicated to the sixty-sixth anniversary of the
Christmas Conference of 1923/24*

Contents

Foreword

The present book is based upon a lecture given by the author at the Vidar Branch of the Anthroposophical Society in Bochum and at the Goetheanum Branch in Dornach on, respectively, 26 February and 5 July 1989 within the context of the general theme of 'Future Aspects of Anthroposophy'.

In response to the numerous requests of listeners and at the suggestion of the publishing house Verlag Freies Geistesleben in Stuttgart, the author decided to present this content in written form, a resolve which entailed a considerable development and deepening of the entire theme.*

Quite apart from the urgency of this particular theme, it will be found that working on it in a spiritual-scientific way—as in the pages of the present work—can serve as yet another clear proof of the truly central significance of Anthroposophy for our time. For it alone has the capacity to answer many of the most burning questions of modern times, and also to give a firm foundation for a real *understanding* of those spiritual-moral forces upon whose development the destiny of the Christ-impulse in our time largely depends. And 'forgiveness' belongs without doubt to those vitally important spiritual-moral forces which must be developed among mankind in the immediate future.

The theme of 'forgiveness' is of particular pertinence to anthroposophists, inasmuch as they have the task of developing a conscious relationship to the central impulses and signs of the age. In

---

* Only when this was completed, the question presented itself to the author as to whether, and if so how, this path of forgiveness related to Rudolf Steiner's own biography. What emerged from investigating this question is contained in Chapter VIII: 'The Manichaean Impulse in the Life of Rudolf Steiner'.

the example of Rudolf Steiner's life path and the Christmas Conference of 1923/24, the significance of this theme may be discerned not only for the past evolution of the Anthroposophical Movement and the Anthroposophical Society but, in particular, for their present and future evolution.

In this sense—and this will be spoken of at further length in the last chapter—we have in the Christmas Conference a shining and deeply rooted archetype for the spiritual evolution in this direction not only of the Anthroposophical Society itself but, in a wider sense, also of humanity as a whole.

To these words, which were written at Christmas 1989, the following should be added as to the way this book came to be written. The question of the occult significance of forgiveness was posed to me in 1988 by Dr Peter Schily (died 1994) from Bochum. He said at the time that this virtue is especially characteristic of the Russian people and that therefore its deeper significance could be demonstrated by someone who was both Russian and an anthroposophist. He also drew my attention to Friedrich Rittelmeyer's book *Das Vaterunser*, where the fifth petition concerning forgiveness is related to our fifth post-Atlantean epoch. I am deeply grateful to Dr Peter Schily for these suggestions.

Sergei O. Prokofieff
1994

I

The Urgency of the Problem of Forgiveness
in our Time

Whoever really knows God will not find it necessary to forgive his brother; he will only have to pardon himself for not having forgiven much sooner!

Leo Tolstoy

If we turn to humanity's path of development in recent times, and especially to the history of the twentieth century—perhaps the most painful and most tragic century in the whole of mankind's earthly existence—we may come to realize the extent to which it is pre-occupied with the problem of 'guilt'.

In our century it has again and again been discussed in all its many aspects, beginning with the 'guilt' of one person towards another and ending with the 'guilt' of one nation with regard to another. The Anthroposophical Society is no exception in this respect, for here, too, there have been debates for years and even decades about the problem of 'guilt' in the tragic events which befell it after the death of Rudolf Steiner, events whose consequences are with us even to this day.

In the great majority of the discussions that have been conducted on this theme both within the Anthroposophical Society and outside it, in the wider world, there has generally been an almost total failure to take into account the counter-pole of the negative conception of 'guilt', namely, the positive conception of *forgiveness*. This circumstance has been particularly associated with the fact that the problem of 'guilt' or 'innocence' is primarily a legal affair while that of 'forgiveness' is an ethical or moral question. Contemporary humanity is, in the present epoch of materialism and one-sided intellectualism, orientated to a considerably greater extent towards abstract legalistic concerns—both in social affairs and in individual conduct—than towards moral or spiritual impulses. In this sense the 'commandments' or 'laws' that are given to an individual or a social group from without play a far greater part in our society than do a person's own moral intuitions which, springing from the innermost part of his being, have their source in that stage of individual development which Rudolf Steiner, in his book *The Philosophy of Freedom*, referred to as 'ethical individualism'.[1]

The attainment of this stage of inner development is, however, connected in a very direct way with the potential for the second, *positive* pole—which was referred to above as that of 'forgiveness'— arising among mankind.

The polarity that we have outlined between the concepts of 'guilt' and 'forgiveness' is at the same time a kind of 'barometer' in their mutual relationship, one which precisely indicates the extent to which a truly Christian impulse is at work in our civilization. One can also say that the contrast between the manner of thinking that is based solely upon the 'commandments' of the Old Testament and the 'laws' of Roman legalism, on the one hand, and the future Christian ideals of freedom and love, on the other, stands before us here with absolute clarity.

Nevertheless, despite the fact that such a state of affairs is so clearly apparent, it has to be said with deep sorrow that the inner forces of *forgiveness* are very feebly developed in the soul of modern man. A major reason for this is that the principle of 'moral preaching' and the 'moral imperative'—which has been practised for centuries among mankind—has increasingly lost its power as the present epoch of the development of the consciousness soul has proceeded. For the consciousness soul necessarily gives rise within man to an overwhelming need not just to blindly surrender oneself or passively follow whatever moral imperative comes towards one from without but, out of a *knowledge* of the deeper spiritual impulses of the age, to find the foundation and the forces for a free and individually moral relationship to oneself and to the world.

It is this central need of modern man to reach also the moral impulses of human evolution through spiritual knowledge that Anthroposophy, the modern science of the spirit, is now called (among much else) to satisfy.

This is why Anthroposophy is so very pertinent to and, one can even say, indispensable for those who, out of a right understanding of the 'signs of the times', are aspiring to keep abreast with the modern stage of the spiritual evolution of the world and of humanity.

II

The Fifth Petition of the Lord's Prayer and the Fifth Post-Atlantean Epoch

And forgive us our debts, as we also have forgiven our debtors.

Matthew 6:12

In order that we may gain a real *understanding* of the problem of forgiveness, by considering it from a more spiritual or occult point of view, we shall begin from its central relationship to the present fifth post-Atlantean cultural epoch.

The prominent anthroposophist and founder of the Christian Community, Friedrich Rittelmeyer, who was one of the closest and most advanced esoteric pupils of Rudolf Steiner, referred to this relationship—which is of extreme importance for the whole of what follows—in a short book that he wrote about the fundamental prayer of Christianity, the Lord's Prayer.[2]

In the first, introductory chapter, entitled 'On Prayer', we find a highly concentrated exposition on the inner relationship that exists between the seven petitions of the Lord's Prayer and the seven post-Atlantean cultural epochs in human evolution. Thus the first post-Atlantean epoch—the Ancient Indian—was founded upon the capacity of the Ancient Indians to see, behind the maya of physical matter, the last glimpses of the great primal revelation of humanity—a direct experience of the activity of the Spirit or the *Name* of the Divine which was hidden everywhere.

The Ancient Persian epoch has as its principal task that of permeating earthly evolution—even to the physical existence of man on Earth—with the forces of the divine *Kingdom* of Light, the forces of the Sun God Ormuzd, in whose countenance the Ancient

Persians, under the leadership of Zarathustra, learnt to recognize the Christ who was to come.

The evolution of the third, Egypto-Babylonian-Assyrian-Chaldean, epoch was under the direction of the priests of the Mysteries, who endeavoured to discern in the regular movements of the moving and fixed stars the *Will* of the higher Gods who rule the universe and, on the basis of this Will, to endow the people entrusted to them with laws capable of directing their personal and social life.

'Only in the Graeco-Roman culture did man wholly arrive on the Earth';[3] a direct consequence of this process in the fourth epoch is the problem of the 'daily bread'. It is a reflection of the new, objective relationship that has been attained by humanity as a whole towards the surrounding earthly world.

Finally, Friedrich Rittelmeyer writes of our fifth cultural epoch: 'German and Anglo-Saxon culture has the task of fully embracing the human ego within the "consciousness-soul". With this a new question, that of personal destiny-struggles, comes strongly to the fore, but it includes also the question of the relationship of one human ego with the egos of other human individuals and the question of the relationship of the human ego with the spiritual world. Man feels himself to be involved more freely and more consciously in the battle between good and evil than hitherto.'

The key to this epoch is the fifth line in the Lord's Prayer: 'And forgive us our debts, as we forgive our debtors'; this is the key to the whole of what will be presented here.

To conclude the sequence, there are the sixth and seventh cultural epochs (the Slavic and the American) which are still to come. The first of these will make the dualism, which has especially from our fifth post-Atlantean epoch onwards become inherent within man for the first time, fully manifest not only inwardly but also in outward social life. What Rudolf Steiner describes as the future division of humanity into two races, the good and the evil, will find its initial embryonic expression in the Slavic epoch.[4] It is significant that in the paintings of the small cupola of the First Goetheanum 'Slavic man' is depicted next to his dark double.[5] Thus this future condition of mankind can best be characterized with the help of the

sixth petition of the Lord's Prayer: 'And lead us not into temptation', that is: Do not allow us to succumb to the dark forces of the
double in us. As for the seventh petition: 'But deliver us from evil',
this is an indication of the fundamental character of the final,
seventh epoch, which will be associated with the beginning of the
'War of All against All', the end of the cycle of the post-Atlantean
epochs and the time before the beginning of a new great period of
earthly evolution.[6]

★

We shall now examine the fifth petition of the Lord's Prayer in
somewhat more detail. Friedrich Rittelmeyer's characterization of
it[7] has already enabled us to see the extent to which this line of the
fundamental prayer of Christianity has a direct relationship to our
time.

There are four problems in particular which may be regarded as
central for our modern age:

— The problem of the ego.
— The problem of social relationships (that is, the relationship of
  one ego to another).
— The problem of a conscious relationship to karma.
— The problem of evil.

All these four problems are intimately connected with the line of
the Lord's Prayer that we are considering here.

Firstly, the problem of the ego is connected with it inasmuch as—
and this will become clear later on—only out of the forces of a fully
evolved ego, such as is made manifest in the consciousness soul and
thereafter seeks the path to the higher ego, can a *true* act of forgiveness be accomplished on the Earth. It is to this relationship of
the lower ego to the higher in the act of forgiveness that the first part
of the fifth petition 'And forgive us our debts . . .' refers. These are
the words with which the lower ego in every individual inwardly
turns to his higher ego.

Secondly, there is the problem of the relationship between ego
and ego, that is, the social problem as such. To this relates not only

the second part of the fifth petition, '. . . as we forgive our debtors', but also Rudolf Steiner's understanding of it. In his lectures on the fundamental prayer of Christianity,[8] he speaks at some length about the connection of the fifth petition of the Lord's Prayer with man's etheric body and, through it, with his social environment. For it is through the particular qualities of the etheric body that the individual enters into connection with one or another social grouping on the Earth, whether it be family, nation or even a whole epoch: 'One belongs to a community because of certain qualities of the etheric body . . . So it is that one's etheric body has the task of adapting itself to other etheric bodies . . . An individual's disharmony with the community represents a shortcoming of the etheric body.'[9] And 'what proceeds from defects in the etheric body is designated by a community as "debt" or "guilt"'.[10] Thus without constant efforts to bring health to social life out of a true spirit of forgiveness, a vital social organism is actually impossible in our present epoch. For any tendency towards vindictiveness or rancour works upon it like a strong poison.

Thirdly, the problem of karma in human life also finds its expression in the line from the Lord's Prayer which we are considering. This is, on the one hand, a person's individual karma as associated with the ego, and, on the other, the karma that connects one person with another throughout earthly evolution—the individual human ego with the social grouping to which he karmically belongs.

And, fourthly, the fifth petition of the Lord's Prayer has a direct relationship to the central problem of the fifth post-Atlantean epoch—that of evil. For just as the principal *inner* problem of the human soul in the fourth post-Atlantean epoch was that of birth and death, together with the need of physical support for the earthly organism throughout the period of earthly life that derives from it ('Give us this day our daily bread'), so the principal *inner* problem of the human soul in the modern, fifth epoch is the encounter with evil and the finding of a right relationship to it.[11] For while the first three petitions of the Lord's Prayer relate to the divine-spiritual world, and the fourth petition to the Earth and to the essential nature of man's physical incarnation thereon, the last three petitions have a direct relationship to the problem of evil and refer to the need for an ever more active and conscious opposition to it. Because only through the conscious struggle with it, a struggle which really only begins with the full flowering of the fifth post-Atlantean epoch—through overcoming the forces of hindrance and evil firstly within himself and then in the outer world—will man gradually be able fully to attain the goal that has been set before him by world evolution, namely, to become, in time, a new Tenth Hierarchy of freedom and love in the cosmos.[12]

This path towards becoming a Tenth Hierarchy, through the successive overcoming of the forces of evil, unfolds in the Lord's Prayer from the fifth petition onwards, which, as we have seen, relates to the present fifth post-Atlantean epoch. It is for this reason that this petition is of such central significance for us, in that it represents the beginning of the path which must in future become the principal path of evolution of Christian humanity if it is eventually truly to attain the goal that has been set before it by the guiding powers of the world. Hence the only line in the Lord's Prayer to which Christ Jesus Himself adds a commentary is this fifth petition. Thus immediately after Christ Jesus has given His disciples the fundamental Christian prayer, He explains it as follows: 'For if you forgive men their trespasses, your heavenly Father also will forgive you; but if you do not forgive men their trespasses, neither will your Father forgive your trespasses' (Matthew 6:14–15).

Moreover, the essential significance which is attached to these words of the prayer in the Gospel is further confirmed by the truly fundamental position that the fifth epoch has in post-Atlantean evolution. For according to the spiritual-scientific research of Rudolf Steiner, 'the fifth culture is the one upon which it all depends; [the path of forgiveness] is something new that has been added, which must be carried over into the sixth age.* The sixth culture will sink into decadence, it will be a culture in decline' (and this will be ever more true of the seventh cultural epoch).[13]

And finally, a consideration of the whole cosmic evolution of the

---

* That is, into the sixth *great* period which will succeed post-Atlantean evolution as a whole.

Earth in the light of the esoteric content of the Lord's Prayer can enable us to view the significance of its fifth petition from yet another aspect. For if we compare the seven petitions of the prayer with cosmic evolution, the following relationships emerge. Its first three petitions about the Name, the Kingdom and the Will are the expression of the principal formative forces of the three previous planetary conditions of the Earth. Thus its Old Saturn condition took place as a consequence of the cosmic sacrifice of the Spirits of *Will*; the foundation of the condition of Old Sun was the establishing by the Spirits of Wisdom of a high Sun *Kingdom* of wisdom, whence they then wielded their authority over the Sun incarnation of our Earth. On Old Moon, with the awakening of imaginative consciousness among earthly humanity,[14] the revelation of the divine *Name* that was being sent down to it from the Sun through the mediation of the Spirits of Movement became ever more accessible in all the beings and processes that surrounded it.

The fourth petition of the Lord's Prayer gives expression to the fundamental tendency of the first half of earthly evolution, which lasts until the Mystery of Golgotha and is primarily under the guidance of the Mars forces. Its task was to lead mankind fully into the world of physical matter, to a direct experience of the meaning of the 'daily bread' for earthly life; while the fifth petition expresses the fundamental tendency of the second, *Christian*, half of earthly evolution, which has the task of leading humanity—through its being permeated by the Christ-impulse—back from the world of matter to the world of spirit, from the world of natural necessity, where 'laws' and 'commandments' alone hold sway, to the full moral freedom and higher paradise which are the fruits of man's conscious striving towards the higher worlds as he gradually ascends from the lower ego to the higher. This ascent will be attained in full measure only at the end of the entire evolution of the present Earth and will then serve as the foundation for its subsequent transition from the Earth aeon (Mercury) to its next cosmic incarnation, the Jupiter aeon. The development within mankind as a whole of the spiritual forces springing from a capacity of true forgiveness is intended to be the beginning of this process.

Here also it should briefly be observed that the most important aspect of the conflict between good and evil that is to take place on Jupiter is to be found in the sixth petition of the Lord's Prayer.[15] Finally, the eventual *cosmic* division between good and evil will ensue on Venus, and it is this that is referred to in the last petition of the prayer.[16]

Thus it follows from what has been said that in the fifth petition of the Lord's Prayer there is not only a guiding principle for the whole of our fifth post-Atlantean epoch but also an indication of the *path* of spiritual ascent which all Christian humanity will tread in the course of the second half of earthly evolution, standing as it does under the sign of Mercury and whose beginning and point of departure is the Mystery of Golgotha.

One of the most important stages of this—the attainment by man of the capacity of true forgiveness—must now be characterized at greater length. It should, however, be pointed out at once that the capacity of forgiveness is neither its first nor, still less, its last or highest stage.

In the modern cycle of earthly evolution, it is possible to distinguish *four* stages of this path, one of which precedes and the other two of which come *after* the stage of 'forgiveness'. It is a path which, through having its source in the Mystery of Golgotha, is not only a Christian path in an ethical or moral sense but—and this is of particular importance for the present epoch—is primarily an occult path of cognition which leads at the same time to a more direct *experience* of the Christ Being and to a deeper *knowledge* of Him. For this alone will enable modern man gradually to become a fully conscious helper and fellow worker of Christ in the process of accomplishing His work on Earth, and that means becoming His *friend* in the sense of those words of His from the Gospel of St John: 'No longer do I call you servants, for the servant does not know what his master is doing; but I have called you friends, for all that I have heard from my Father I have made known to you' (15:15).

According to these words, the chief difference between the 'servants' of Christ and His 'friends' is that the former are still guided solely by 'laws' and 'commandments' given to them from without, while the distinguishing trait of the latter is first and foremost the *knowledge* of what Christ expects from us in every new period of earthly evolution; for us this means what He expects now in this fifth post-Atlantean cultural epoch. But this is precisely what Anthroposophy, with its proclamation of the central spiritual event of our time—the appearance of Christ in the etheric body—is now called upon to impart to mankind.

In this sense, Anthroposophy can be seen not only as the sum of definite knowledge about the spiritual worlds but as a *real language* whereby people of today can turn directly to the Etheric Christ— who is working among mankind even now—in order to ask Him about the most important things that He has 'heard from the Father' *with regard to our own epoch*. Rudolf Steiner refers to this central significance of Anthroposophy, or the modern science of the spirit, in the following words: 'So let us try to make spiritual science our own not merely as a teaching but as a language, and then wait until we find in this language the questions which we may address to Christ. He will answer, yes, He *will* answer! And abundant will be the soul forces, the soul invigoration, the soul impulses, that will be borne away by those who, out of the grey spiritual depths that are characteristic of the present phase of human evolution, will receive instruction from Christ—and in the near future He will give this to those that seek it.'[17] For in our time it is the quest for such a conscious relationship to the new revelation of Christ in the etheric realm, with all the spiritual and social tasks that issue from it, that can alone make a *human individual of today* in a real sense a *friend* of Christ.

And the most important capacity which man must inwardly develop—apart from the study of spiritual science, the spiritual language in which the Etheric Christ wishes to speak to the modern human soul—is that of *true forgiveness*, a capacity which, as will be shown later, has in its occult nature a quite particular relationship to the experience of the Etheric Christ and is at the same time one part of the path which leads from His modern etheric revelation to His still higher revelation in the future.

However, before turning to a more detailed description of the path that we have been outlining, and also to a fuller consideration of the occult foundations and the spiritual nature of the process of *forgiveness*, it is necessary that we indicate its significance for the modern epoch by means of concrete examples, which will enable us truly to sense to what extent mankind needs forgiveness no longer in the form of abstract preaching but as direct spiritual-scientific *knowledge.*

III

Seven Examples of Forgiveness

The problem of forgiveness is raised, in perhaps the most acute and direct form for our time, in Simon Wiesenthal's book *The Sunflower. A Tale of Guilt and Forgiveness.*[18] The story that is recounted in this unusual book is as follows. During the Second World War the author of the book was in the Nazi concentration camp in Lemberg. The life-conditions in the camp were terrible. Each day people were beaten and shot dead, work from morning till night surpassed people's strength, and hunger prevailed. The slightest act of insubordination would cost one one's life, and illness and exhaustion led inevitably to death.

It came about that the group of prisoners to which Simon Wiesenthal belonged was sent to work at a field hospital not far from the camp, in what had formerly been Lemberg's Technical College. In the course of this work a nurse came up to Wiesenthal and, having asked him if he was a Jew, invited him to go with her into one of the wards. She led him into a small, barely lit room where she left him alone at the bedside of an invalid who was bandaged from head to foot, so that apart from his lips, nose and emaciated hands it was impossible to see anything of him at all. And then from the lips of this dying man Simon Wiesenthal, who was himself at every moment in mortal danger, heard the following confession.

Before him lay a man who was still young, no more than 21 years old. He was a German, but already in early youth, having fallen prey to Nazi propaganda, he first entered the Hitler Youth Movement and then—of his own accord—the forces of the SS, shortly after which he was sent to the Eastern Front.

The crime that the dying man wanted to impart to the Jewish prisoner was enacted in the Ukrainian town of Dnyepropetrovsk. Upon abandoning the town, the Russians had mined many of the houses and streets. Explosions occurred in the town, and several of the soldiers of the German army were killed or wounded. Vengeance was not long in coming. The same day the SS subdivision in which the youth served was sent to the other end of the town, where the appalling crime took place. Between one hundred and fifty and two hundred Jewish prisoners, who were drawn from the non-military population of the town and included many women, children and old people, were driven by force into a small building, in whose upper storeys tanks of petrol had been planted. The doors of the house were firmly shut and the SS soldiers standing outside around the house were ordered to ignite the petrol by shooting at the tanks and then to shoot anyone who tried to escape by jumping from a window. And there were many who tried to escape from the blazing inferno in this way.

One image in particular was engraved in the memory of the dying man: that of a man holding a child in his arms. His clothes already alight, he covers the child's eyes and jumps with it from the window. The mother jumps down immediately after them.

'We opened fire, but I shall never forget this family, especially the child . . .'—with these words the dying man ended his terrible story.

After perpetrating this crime the SS subdivision to which he belonged was sent to the south. There was heavy fighting in the region of southern Ukraine and in Crimea. However, the memory of the crime gave him no peace. 'It was some time before I became aware of how much guilt I had incurred.'

Only gradually did what he expressed to his guest in the words 'I wasn't born a murderer, I have made myself a murderer' become wholly clear to him. But shortly after the awareness of what he had done awoke with full force in his soul, the following incident took place during an attack. The dying man described to Simon Wiesenthal what happened to him in the following words: 'But suddenly I stood still as though rooted to the spot. Something was approaching me. My hands, which were holding a rifle with fixed bayonet, began to tremble. And then I saw with total clarity the burning family, the father with the child and the mother behind them—and they were coming towards me. "No, I won't shoot them a second time," the thought flashed through my head ... And then a grenade exploded beside me. I lost consciousness. When I came to my senses in the sickbay, I realized that I was blind. My whole face is mutilated, and the upper part of my body has also been heavily hit. I consist of nothing but wounds. A sister told me that the doctor has taken a whole bucket of grenade splinters out of my body. It is a miracle that I am still alive—I am as good as dead ...'

However, these immense physical sufferings were nothing in comparison with the unendurable moral torments and pangs of remorse which, now that he had recovered consciousness, he was experiencing day and night without any interruption, like a slow torture which did not cease for a single moment: 'But my conscience torments me far more than this. The burning house and the family jumping out of the window leave me no peace.'

And finally, after a brief pause, the dying man uttered the following decisive words: 'I know that what I have told you is terrible. In the long nights that I have spent waiting for death, I have had ever and again the need to speak with a Jew about it ... and ask his forgiveness ... I know that what I am asking is almost too much for you. But without an answer I cannot die in peace.'

After these last words there was silence. The question that had been posed had a truly fundamental significance not just for the two men in that room but, indeed, for all mankind and for its future evolution. However, for the two whom destiny had so strangely brought together there, the question could not be resolved. And Simon Wiesenthal, in silence and without saying a word in reply, left the room. The following day, when he arrived for work at the sickbay, he learnt that the youth who had spoken with him the day before had died that night. Thus the story found—or so it would appear—its natural ending.

Nevertheless, for Simon Wiesenthal this was by no means the case. As the very fact that he describes it in his book testifies, it was this apparently 'insignificant' episode which—even when compared with all the horrors and sufferings that he witnessed and experienced in the camp—came after the passage of many years to represent for him in a certain sense the central moral problem of his life. A man who had passed through the terrible hell of several Nazi concentration camps, was accustomed to look death in the face every day and had on more than one occasion witnessed the innocent death of tens and even hundreds of men, women, children and old people, a man who then devoted his later life to the search for Nazi criminals so that they might be handed over to earthly justice: this courageous and truly fearless man was rendered completely powerless when confronted by the moral problem posed to him by his destiny, a problem which in a certain sense stands before the whole of humanity.

One can also say that, through the veil of the personal karma of Simon Wiesenthal, something has been manifested which touches upon the very essence of the karma of contemporary humanity. Thus it is out of a wholly right inner feeling that in his search for a resolution of the problem that confronts him he has directed his tale to *all* men and women. The second half of his book consists of a whole series of observations that reflect the many attempts on the part of a great variety of people to resolve this problem.

However, if one familiarizes oneself with all these many attempts, the feeling arises again and again that the *level* at which they are undertaken in itself dooms them in advance to failure. Indeed, the arguments 'for' and 'against' forgiveness that are adduced on *this* level soon form a kind of enclosed circle from which there is no way out. A person can surely forgive only on his own behalf. Can he really forgive on behalf of others? Or: as a Christian I consider that the author of the story should have forgiven the dying man in view of his repentence. But as the author does not profess the Christian faith, the problem again turns out to be insoluble, and so on. One could easily cite here a number of similar lines of argument from the second half of the book.

Thus if one reads all the readers' letters quoted in the book it is impossible to shake off the impression that it is in this very question as perhaps in no other that, on the one hand, a certain spiritual weakness of present-day humanity is manifested and, on the other, that this is a question to which—and this becomes a firm conviction—spiritual science or Anthroposophy can and must have something to say. It has the task of speaking forth out of that wholly different level of understanding of man's being—his life and his destiny (karma)—which can in our time spring only from the fruits of true spiritual research.

In any event, it is quite clear from the story related by Simon Wiesenthal that the problem of guilt and forgiveness, which is alluded to in the subtitle to his book, is indeed a central problem of our time.

★

As a second example, forming a kind of polar opposite to the first, we shall now consider a story described by the American psychiatrist, George G. Ritchie, in his book *Return from Tomorrow.*[19] The principal theme of his book is a supersensible experience that the author had at the end of 1943 in the military camp where he, as a 20-year-old recruit, was undergoing training for subsequent participation—in the ranks of the American army—in the Second World War.

Having succumbed at the military camp to a serious attack of pneumonia, which led to his being for some time on the threshold between life and death, George Ritchie had a series of supersensible experiences outside his physical body. These experiences, despite their often being of an exaggeratedly material, earthly nature, a consequence of the total unpreparedness of George Ritchie's consciousness for receiving them, and also of the extreme distance that his life had been removed from any spiritual interests before the illness, nevertheless from an anthroposophical point of view contain—not necessarily always in their form but at any rate in their content—much that is true.

The central focus of the many clairvoyant experiences of the author that are described in the book and also their culmination is without doubt his supersensible meeting with the Etheric Christ in the spiritual world adjoining the earthly sphere.

It is not the task of the present work to give a detailed exposition of George Ritchie's encounter with the supersensible Christ but rather to offer a commentary on his description. Suffice it to say that this experience was decisive for the whole of his life thereafter and quite fundamentally changed its course. From being a typically modern, materialistically inclined young man, George Ritchie became for the rest of his life a Christian in the deepest sense, personally convinced of the fundamental truths of Christianity not out of some religious tradition but directly from the spiritual world itself.

However, the supersensible experience which was, through his karma, granted to George Ritchie had for him another quite different consequence. For after this, without doubt the central moment in his life, when Christ Himself appeared to him in a clairvoyant vision, there was no wish that filled his soul with such strength as did the wish to experience another supersensible meeting with Him: 'The lonesomeness I had felt that year, the alienation from the world and the things that went on here—wasn't it all a longing to go back to the time when I had stood in His Presence?' writes Ritchie in his book.

George Ritchie had, however, to live many more months with this request in his soul, this question to the spiritual world until, over a year after his supersensible meeting with Christ, from the spiritual world itself there came an answer which gave him an indication of the possibility of a further, and altogether different, experience of Christ, the aspiration towards which was thenceforth to become the most important element of his subsequent life. He describes this new knowledge as follows: 'It was no good, I suddenly saw, looking for Him in the past, even when that past was only fifteen months before. I knew that afternoon, on the road from Rethel, that if I wanted to feel the nearness of Christ—and I did want that, above everything else—I would have to find it *in the people* that He put before me each day.' This was for George Ritchie a completely new path to Christ, and he speaks about its beginning with the American straightforwardness that is characteristic of him: 'The first step, I realized, was to stop trying to recapture that otherworldly vision of Jesus, and start looking for him in the faces across the mess table.'

And then in his book he cites several instances of such a direct experience of Christ *through the other people* that he meets. For the most part these were meetings with people of whom, in recollection of his clairvoyant experience, he could say with absolute certainty: Yes, through the eyes of this person standing before me Christ Himself is looking at me, and in the features of the face of this person the Countenance of Christ Himself is manifested to me. Moreover, the extent to which the other person whom George Ritchie met in this way was actually conscious of this had no decisive significance.

Of the encounters described by George Ritchie, there is one in particular which has an absolutely direct relationship to our theme. This took place in May 1945, at the very end of the war, when Ritchie was sent as one of a small group of doctors to a Nazi concentration camp that had just been liberated, on German territory not far from Wuppertal, in order to give urgent medical help to the prisoners who had been found there. Thousands of people from various European countries, many of whom were Jews, were all on the verge of starvation. Many of them were beyond help. Thus despite all the medical efforts and improved nutrition, people continued to die by the score every day. For Ritchie, what he witnessed in the camp was worse than all the most terrible experiences of the war. However, now that he had received an answer to the question which for him was most important, he endeavoured also in this new trial to discover everywhere the mysterious presence of Christ. He writes of this as follows: 'Now I needed my new insight, indeed. When the ugliness became too great to handle I did what I had learned to do. I went from one end to the other of that barbed wire enclosure looking into men's faces until I saw looking back at me the face of Christ.' And then he continues: 'And that's how I came to know Wild Bill Cody'. That wasn't his real name. He was called that for simplicity's sake by the American soldiers. In origin he was a Polish Jew, but George Ritchie could barely decipher his real name in his papers and finally was no longer able to remember it. However, what had struck him from the very beginning was the wholly incomprehensible fact that when compared with all the other prisoners in the camp—most of whom were hardly able to walk—Bill Cody looked quite different: 'his posture was erect, his eyes bright, his energy indefatigable.' And as he spoke five different languages and was a kind of unofficial camp interpreter, his help in sorting out the paperwork and in

ascertaining the identities of the living and the dead was indispensable. However, Ritchie's amazement became even greater
when he became more closely acquainted with the way that Bill
Cody worked. This is what he writes about this process: 'But
though Wild Bill worked 15 and 16 hours a day, he showed no signs
of weariness. While the rest of us were dropping with fatigue, he
seemed to gain strength. "We have time for this old fellow," he'd
say. "He's been waiting to see us all day." His compassion for his
fellow-prisoners glowed on his face, and it was to this glow that I
came when my own spirits were low.'

In the end, George Ritchie was unable to find any other
explanation for these unusual physical and soul forces of Bill Cody
than the supposition that he must, after all, unlike all the other
prisoners in the camp, have been in the camp for only a short time.
How great must have been his amazement when he discovered
from Bill Cody's papers, which were kept in the camp archives, that
this man had already spent *six* years at the camp: 'So I was astonished
to learn when Wild Bill's own papers came before us one day that
he had been in Wuppertal since 1939! For six years he had lived on
the same starvation diet, slept in the same airless and disease-ridden
barracks as everyone else, but without the least physical or mental
deterioration. Perhaps even more amazing, every group in the camp
looked on him as a friend. He was the one to whom quarrels
between inmates were brought for arbitration. Only after I'd been
at Wuppertal a number of weeks did I realize what a rarity this was
in a compound where the different nationalities of prisoners hated
each other almost as much as they did the Germans.' And in all the
many situations of acute conflict which arose ever and again in the
camp and also beyond its bounds, '... again Wild Bill was our
greatest asset,' writes Ritchie, 'reasoning with the different groups,
counselling forgiveness.'

For quite some time the riddle of this unusual man remained
unsolvable for George Ritchie, until one day, in response to an
observation of his that it is so difficult for people who have endured
imprisonment and all the horrors of the camp to forgive, because so
many of them have lost members of their families in the camps, Bill
Cody finally related his own story.

This brief account is truly one of the most remarkable human testimonies of the potential of the power of forgiveness. Because of its extreme importance for our forthcoming discussion, it will be quoted here in full as it is reported in George Ritchie's book.

' "We lived in the Jewish section of Warsaw," he began slowly, the first words I had heard him speak about himself, "my wife, our two daughters, and our three little boys. When the Germans reached our street they lined everyone against a wall and opened up with machine guns. I begged to be allowed to die with my family, but because I spoke German they put me in a work group."

'He paused, perhaps seeing again his wife and five children. "I had to decide right then," he continued, "whether to let myself hate the soldiers who had done this. It was an easy decision, really. I was a lawyer. In my practice I had seen too often what hate could do to people's minds and bodies. Hate had just killed the six people who mattered most to me in the world. I decided then that I would spend the rest of my life—whether it was a few days or many years—loving every person I came in contact with." '

And Ritchie adds to this inexpressibly tragic story the following words of his own: 'Loving every person . . . this was the power that had kept a man well in the face of every privation. It was the Power I had first met in a hospital room in Texas, and was learning little by little to recognize wherever He chose to shine through—whether the human vehicle was aware of Him or not.'

There are two aspects of this story which have a particular significance for the further exposition of our theme. Firstly, the astonishing and, at first sight, altogether incomprehensible words of Bill that the decision to forgive 'was an easy decision really', and then the second decision that he took together with the first of 'loving every person I came in contact with'. We shall speak later on about the soul forces out of which alone this 'easy' decision could have been taken and about the occult significance of the second decision.

★

Before turning to examples of forgiveness which are directly associated with the history of the Anthroposophical Society in our century, we shall first consider an example from the history of nineteenth-century Russia which has a bearing upon the significance of the impulse of forgiveness not only for the destiny of individual human beings or societies but also for whole nations.

On 1 March 1881 in Petersburg, Tsar Alexander II was murdered by a group of revolutionary terrorists. The court condemned the five regicides—one of whom was a woman—to death by hanging. The public execution of the condemned was to take place on 3 April that same year. However, the last word—at the very end of the judicial process and after the passing of sentence—belonged to the son of the murdered Tsar, Alexander III, who had only just ascended the throne. According to the law, he alone had the right to pardon the criminals at the last moment or to enact the sentence of the court.

At that time, two of the leading representatives of the cultural life of Russia in the second half of the nineteenth century made direct appeals—almost at the same time and without mutual knowledge—to the Tsar for mercy for those who had been condemned. These men were Vladimir Solovyov and Leo Tolstoy. Solovyov first gave a public lecture on this theme in the hall of the Petersburg Credit Society, after which he was forbidden to teach any longer at the university or give any public address. As he feared that the content of the lecture had been communicated to the Tsar in a distorted form, Solovyov sent him a personal letter in which he wrote the following: 'Believing that only the spiritual power of the truth of Christ can conquer the power of evil and destruction which is manifesting itself now to so unprecedented a degree, believing also that the Russian nation in its entirety lives and moves by the Spirit of Christ, believing finally that the Tsar of Russia is the representative and the expression of the Folk Spirit, the bearer of all the best forces of the nation, I resolved to confess this faith of mine from a public rostrum. At the end of my speech I said that the present painful time will give the Russian Tsar an unprecedented opportunity to display the power of the Christian principle of all-forgiveness and thereby to accomplish a supreme moral deed which will exalt his authority to a height never previously reached and consolidate his power upon a thoroughly firm foundation. By

showing mercy to the enemies of his authority, despite all the
natural feelings of the human heart, all the calculations and considerations of earthly wisdom, the Tsar will become exalted to a
superhuman height, and by this deed will show the divine significance of the Tsar's authority; he will show that he is invested
with the highest spiritual power of the entire Russian people,
because there is no one among this whole nation who would be
able to accomplish more for the future.'[20]

Independently of Solovyov, Leo Tolstoy also addressed the
young Tsar with a letter. Unfortunately, the original of the letter has
not been preserved and its content is known only through a rough
draft left by the author. Here, the 53-year-old world-famous writer
turns to Alexander III—as he puts it—not as to a 'lord' but 'simply
as one man to another.'[21] And then, drawing upon the Gospels,
Tolstoy calls the wish of the Tsar to exact earthly retribution and
authorize a new murder, guided only by the interests of the State,
'the most terrible temptation', while to forgive the murderers
would mean overcoming it: '... and you (if you forgive) will have
achieved the greatest deed in the world, you will have overcome
temptation, and you, Tsar, will have given the world a supreme
example of the fulfilment of Christ's teaching of returning good for
evil.' And then Tolstoy continues: 'If you do not forgive, if you
execute the criminals, you will manage to exterminate three or four
out of a number of hundreds, but evil begets evil and instead of
three or four there will be 30 or 40, and you will have lost forever
that moment which alone is more precious than a whole century—
the moment when you could have fulfilled the will of God and you
did not do so; and you will have passed by forever that crossroads at
which you could have chosen good instead of evil, and will be
bound up forever with the affairs of evil, otherwise known as the
public good ... If you forgive, if you render good for evil, out of
hundreds of villains a few score will turn neither to you, nor to them
(this is of no importance) but will turn from the devil to God, and
thousands and millions of hearts will beat for joy and tender
emotion at the sight of the example of good from the throne at so
terrible a moment for the son of a murdered father. My lord, if you
have done this ... and have written a manifesto headed with the

words: and I say to you, love your enemies ... I know how much goodness and love will stream through Russia as a result of these words. The truths of Christ are alive in the hearts of men, and only they are alive, and we love others only in the name of these truths.'

In these words, Leo Tolstoy expresses that truly prophetic feeling of his, which then becomes an invincible sense of certainty, that answering evil with evil, and blood with blood, will in itself never bring healing to Russia but will on the contrary inevitably entail the revenge of dark forces, which is to say, new evil and new blood— 'instead of three or four there will be 30 or 40 and a relentlessly revolving bloody wheel will sooner or later be the ruin of Christian Russia.' Thus for Tolstoy, '... it is not the number [of revolutionaries] that is important, it is not a question of destroying or exiling them in ever greater numbers but of destroying their leaven, of *giving a different leaven.*'

'What are revolutionaries?' he continues in his letter to the Tsar. 'They are people who hate the existing order of things, they find it bad and have in their minds the foundations for a future state of affairs which will be better. You can kill them and destroy them, but you cannot fight them. It is not their number that is important but *rather their thoughts.* In order to fight them, one needs to fight spiritually. Their ideal is sufficiency for all, equality and freedom. In order to fight them, it is necessary to place over and against them an ideal such as would be higher than their ideal and would include their ideal ... There is only one ideal which can withstand them. And the ideal from which theirs is derived, although they do not understand it and so blaspheme against it, the ideal which includes their ideal, is that of love, forgiveness and rendering good for evil. Only one word of forgiveness and Christian love, pronounced and fulfilled from the heights of the throne, and the path of the Christian reign which you are about to embark upon can destroy that evil which is preying upon Russia.'

As we read these words now after more than a century, it is impossible not to be struck by their remarkable prophetic significance and at the same time by Tolstoy's (and, moreover, also Solovyov's) profound understanding of those moral weaknesses, together with the shortcomings to which they gave rise, of the ruling stratum of Russian society which were the ground within which the poisonous shoot of Bolshevism was able to take root and yield its bloody fruits.

Alexander III, as we know, was unable to rise to the moral heights that were necessary. Under the influence of his closest advisers, he did not heed the voice of the higher national conscience which spoke to him through Solovyov and Tolstoy. Thus at the last moment before the impending downfall of the Empire, the ideal of a Christian Tsar who was the true representative of the Christ-people turned out to be beyond the reach of the morally impaired and decadent Romanov dynasty. Alexander III did not even answer the letters sent to him by the great Russian philosopher and the great Russian writer but merely 'decreed ... that Solovyov ... be reprimanded for the inappropriate judgements which he uttered in his public lecture' and that Count Leo Nikolayevich Tolstoy '... be told that if an attempt had been made on his own life he might indeed forgive, but he would have no right to forgive the murderer of his father.'[22]

Nevertheless, if we look back from our time we can say with some certainty that what these great geniuses of nineteenth-century Russia were summoning the last-but-one Russian Tsar to do represented perhaps the last real opportunity, the last chance, of preventing the great empire of evil from becoming established in Eastern Europe in the first quarter of the twentieth century.[23] Thus 37 years later the last Russian Tsar, and the whole of Russia, had to pay so cruelly for the moral weakness of his predecessor, for the refusal to follow the advice of the two representatives of the true spirit of the Russian people, for the refusal *to forgive*, that is, for the refusal to remain true to Russia's higher spiritual calling. For if a higher act of forgiveness had been accomplished at that time, this would without doubt have led to so considerable a strengthening of the Tsar's moral authority among the people, an authority which had by that time greatly declined, that the Bolsheviks when they appeared only two decades later would simply not have found around them a suitable environment for the fulfilment of their plans.

This is, therefore, an example which shows with particular clarity that the question of forgiveness can prove to be decisive for the destiny of a whole nation, and to some extent also for the whole of humanity throughout virtually an entire century.

★

If we now turn to the history of the Anthroposophical Movement and the Anthroposophical Society in the twentieth century, and particularly to the deeply tragic events in its evolution after Rudolf Steiner's death, and if we familiarize ourselves with all the memoirs, polemical articles, letters, stenograms of speeches, minutes of meetings, etc. devoted to these events, there is one document among the great diversity of these materials that stands out as being of particular importance for our theme. For in this document, as distinct from the overwhelming majority of similar treatises, the main emphasis is not upon the negative concept of 'guilt' but upon the positive concept of 'forgiveness'; instead of dwelling upon a quest for who is to blame, which by its nature is directed only to the past and is from a spiritual point of view completely fruitless, it speaks about a different and uniquely fruitful path which is capable of leading into the future out of the spirit of Anthroposophy.

This document is the 'Versöhnungsappell' ('An Appeal for Reconciliation') published by Marie Steiner in the *Nachrichtenblatt* ('Newsheet') for members of the Anthroposophical Society on 12 December 1942.[24]

What, then, did Marie Steiner see as—in her words—the only solution to the profoundly tragic situation that had arisen at that time in the Anthroposophical Society? She saw that the surest way of resolving the many problems of the Anthroposophical Society must be the strengthening, in every possible way, of its moral substance. Such an achievement would be made possible in the first instance by a deed of true forgiveness. Marie Steiner writes about this in her 'Appeal': 'And yet miracles can still happen. They happen when the moral substance is of such strength that it can make a miracle possible. What can we do to rescue our moral substance?

'We can forgive! Everyone can forgive what lies within him to forgive. We can forget what ought to be forgotten instead of rummaging about among old injustices. We could draw a line beneath all the old stories that wear us down and which, either because we are young or are no longer involved, we are not in a position to get to the bottom of.'

Such an act of forgiveness (in the highest and truest sense of the word) can, according to Marie Steiner, indeed fulfil a condition of this kind. She refers to this *fundamental condition* with all the clarity that belongs to her nature: 'The resolve to *overcome oneself* should be consciously taken hold of by the community. Clearly and willingly.' And then at the very end of her 'Appeal', turning to all the members of the Anthroposophical Society, she writes: 'Let us rescue his [Rudolf Steiner's] work and human culture by overcoming ourselves and achieving reconciliation, by opening our gates wide to those who seek them.'

As we read these words and become imbued with the spiritual content that lies behind them, the strong feeling arises that if the moral substance that they contain had at that critical moment been taken up by a greater number of anthroposophically inclined souls, and if the voice that sounds through them had been heard by a greater number of hearts sincerely beating for Anthroposophy, the last and most serious catastrophe in the history of the Anthroposophical Society, the consequences of which have not been fully overcome even to this day, might not have occurred. Moreover, in this eventuality the whole subsequent destiny of the Anthroposophical Society might have turned out completely differently.

This document arouses a particularly strong impression because Marie Steiner characterizes it as a spiritual testament which she was leaving to all members of the Anthroposophical Society and in the first place, of course, to her closest friends and colleagues. She writes about this as follows: 'It seems to me that this [forgetting and forgiving] offers us the only possibility for our purification—as a society and as individuals. I say this in full awareness of the fact that in human estimation I shall shortly have to appear before Rudolf Steiner's spiritual form.'[25]

It is perhaps one of the gravest features of the history of the Anthroposophical Society since Rudolf Steiner's death that this 'Appeal' has not as yet been sufficiently heard by the members of the

Anthroposophical Society. Curiously, it was not really even heard by the friends and followers of Marie Steiner. Even among them there were not enough people, either at the time or later, who wholly acknowledged the inner moral impulse of this 'spiritual testament' by the closest colleague of Rudolf Steiner, and tried to transform it into a reality.

Thus Marie Steiner's 'Appeal' tragically remained unheard for several decades and her spiritual will still awaits its final fulfilment. For the significance and spiritual content of this 'Appeal' has not in the least degree lost its power or relevance in our time, inasmuch as—and this will be shown later on—its moral substance truly springs from the central spiritual impulse of Anthroposophy.

At that time (in 1942) there were two people in particular who experienced with marked intensity the spiritual impulse that stood *behind* this 'Appeal'. The first person was the other closest colleague of Rudolf Steiner, Ita Wegman, who in her letter to Marie Steiner applied to it the words 'great and full of possibilities for the future',[26] and the second, the well-known Swiss anthroposophist F. Eymann, who when he read it took the decision just at that critical moment to become a member of the Anthroposophical Society.

★

If we would now understand at a somewhat deeper level the spiritual sources from which Marie Steiner was able to derive the impulse for drawing up this 'Appeal'—and in order to write it she must in the first place have found within herself forces which enabled her to forgive—it is necessary that we turn to a further, quite central, example of forgiveness in the history of the Anthroposophical Movement and the Anthroposophical Society. This example, which stands before all the members of the Anthroposophical Society as a kind of higher archetype, is Rudolf Steiner's deed at the Christmas Conference of 1923/24. This will be spoken of at greater length in Part Two of the present work. At this point it will only be touched upon quite briefly.

Let us first look at the deeply tragic situation of the last years of Rudolf Steiner's life and work, in particular the year which preceded the Christmas Conference, 1923. The impulse to establish a threefold social order in 1918–19 had failed, with far-reaching consequences for the historical destiny of Central and, in a wider sense, the whole of Europe.[27] The two *Hochschulkurse* in the First Goetheanum (in 1920 and 1921) were by virtue of their content—in Rudolf Steiner's words—in many respects totally at variance with the spirit of the building. For in them, instead of science being fructified by Anthroposophy the reverse took place: Anthroposophy was everywhere invaded by natural-scientific habits of thinking. The so-called 'Stuttgart system' was gradually formed, which became in time a bureaucratic wall separating Rudolf Steiner to an ever-increasing degree from the members of the Society and making his direct contact with them more and more difficult. Finally, the Goetheanum's destruction by fire was a frightening symptom of the ever-growing split in the Anthroposophical Society itself. Thus the ruins on the Dornach hill in 1923 were also a visible symbol of the ruins of the Anthroposophical Society, as Rudolf Steiner indicated in the introductory lecture on the first day of the Christmas Conference.

The underlying cause of these, and also of many other tragic events, was—apart from the extreme hostility that was being renewed from without—an ever-increasing number of errors that were being made in all kinds of areas by the members of the Anthroposophical Society themselves, in the majority of cases out of an inadequately trained faculty of judgement and out of personal ambition. Rudolf Steiner once spoke about this as follows: 'I shall be made responsible for all the errors of the Society, and the Movement will suffer as a result.'[28]

Moreover, from the beginning of the twenties and even earlier a kind of 'inner opposition' had gradually begun to form among the members of the Anthroposophical Society that was directed against Rudolf Steiner himself and, hence, against the anthroposophical impulse for which he stood. Especially during 1923, Rudolf Steiner again and again referred to this inner opposition, for example, in the penultimate lecture of the cycle that he gave in the summer of 1923 in Dornach with the title 'The History and Circumstances of the Anthroposophical Movement in Relation to the Anthroposophical

Society':[29] 'In this third period [1918–23] there began to form what I might call an inner opposition towards my particular involvement in the Anthroposophical Society, a certain inner opposition. Naturally, most people are astonished when I speak of this inner opposition, because they—at any rate many of them—are not aware of it. But I would say: so much the worse for them. For this inner opposition has just in this third period begun to work very strongly in the realm of feeling.'[30]

By the year 1923 the general situation in the Anthroposophical Society for Rudolf Steiner and his own position within it had altogether become so unendurable that he even became seriously inclined to leave it completely and continue his work only in private, with a very small circle of his most faithful and advanced pupils. It is true that in private conversations Rudolf Steiner had already mentioned such a possibility considerably earlier. Marie Steiner made the following recollection in this regard in 1926: 'In the aftermath of the war, in many a difficult moment of failure before the hatefully inspired struggle of the adversaries, and of indifference before their destructive zeal, Rudolf Steiner had often spoken out in such terms: "Who knows whether it might not be better to carry the Movement forward without the Society".'[31] However, this state of affairs reached its culmination in 1923. Already in April, at the general gathering of the Anthoposophical Society in Switzerland, Rudolf Steiner indicated clearly that if essential changes did not take place in the Society in the immediate future and everything were to remain as before, this would make it necessary 'for me to discontinue my activity for the Anthroposophical Society and to withdraw to a task of a purely personal nature.'[32]

Then in November of the same year, during his stay in The Hague for the occasion of the founding of the Dutch National Society, Rudolf Steiner, in the presence of a large number of leading Dutch anthroposophists, uttered the following words with an undisguised bitterness, almost in despair: 'The members do not want it . . . they are full of good intentions, but . . . What am I to do? Shall I found an order?!'[33] Willem Zeylmans van Emmichoven, who was present, continues his description of this evening in the following words: 'We sat there completely shattered; we could not help feeling what a profound grief had filled him and what a heavy burden of care had come to rest on his shoulders. Only very slowly did the conversation get going again, and Dr Steiner explained more clearly the extent to which he was everywhere and ever and again disappointed by the Society, and what he found lacking in it. He also said that he had given quite definite suggestions . . . and now instead of taking hold of what was suggested people came along with quite different, wholly inadequate, proposals . . .'

The gravity with which Rudolf Steiner thought about this during 1923 can be discerned from the fact that when he came to look back at what had happened he considered it necessary to mention this possibility in his address at the opening of the Christmas Conference: 'It is indeed the case that things must now be taken very seriously, in bitter earnest, otherwise what I have often spoken about—that I would have to withdraw from the Anthroposophical Society—would actually have to come about.'[34]

And yet, despite all this, Rudolf Steiner did not arrive at this step but instead accomplished the direct opposite, namely, having taken upon himself the office of President at the Christmas Conference, he united his destiny fully and without reservation with the destiny of the General Anthoposophical Society. That is to say, he received *all* the members of the newly founded Society into the sphere of his own karma, *including those who were inwardly opposed to him*. Here we have something which we should place with all possible clarity before our moral consciousness, namely, that at the Christmas Conference Rudolf Steiner took the decision not to drive 'opposition' out of the Society, not to shun it by leaving everyone to their own devices, but on the contrary, by uniting himself with the Society *united himself also with the opposition!* And from the occult point of view this was possible only through making the *principle of forgiveness* a reality in the highest Christian sense, forgiving all the members of the Anthoposophical Society for *all* their previous mistakes and even for their opposition towards himself, the consequences of which actions and attitudes Rudolf Steiner had ever and again to bear personally in both an outer and an inner sense.

This act of complete and unreserved forgiveness which Rudolf

Steiner achieved on the eve of the Christmas Conference formed the actual spiritual substance, the spiritual-moral soil out of which alone the impulse of the Christmas Conference, the modern impulse of the new Christian Mysteries, was subsequently able to grow.

It was out of these deep foundations, out of this central anthroposophical impulse, that Marie Steiner wrote her 'Appeal for Reconciliation' in 1942. And it was in this same sense that, until the very end of her life, she understood the idea and the tasks of the 'esoteric *Vorstand*' that Rudolf Steiner had convened: 'It could be an esotericism of the deepest kind to bring hitherto diverging earlier spiritual streams into harmonious equilibrium through certain of their present representatives,' she wrote in this connection in 1944 in the foreword to the first edition of the complete stenographical report of the Christmas Conference.[35]

The realization of this 'harmonious equilibrium', as in the past so also in our time and most especially in the future, will be possible only through preserving and strengthening that 'moral substance' which is attainable solely through the qualities of forgiveness, willingness to forget, and reconciliation that have their roots in the capacity to overcome oneself; these were the qualities which Marie Steiner sought above all to call forth through her 'Appeal' of 1942.

From this it becomes understandable why out of Rudolf Steiner's closest colleagues this 'Appeal' made so 'deep an impression' on Ita Wegman, whose question to Rudolf Steiner about the 'new Mysteries' played so important a part in his final decision to inaugurate the Christmas Conference. For in Marie Steiner's words Ita Wegman saw not only a means of addressing the moral consciousness of those members of the Society 'who are true to the work and to Rudolf Steiner' but above all a living presence and a concrete manifestation of the central *impulse of the Christmas Conference*. It is in this deeper sense alone that we may rightly understand Ita Wegman's observation that the words of Marie Steiner's 'Appeal' 'are great and full of possibilities for the future'. However, they will only be such if people are found in the Anthroposophical Society who through a genuine spirit of *self-overcoming* have the wish to bring them to a real fulfilment!

One of the examples of such a fulfilment of these words, that is, of a deed accomplished out of the central impulse of the Christmas Conference, is Zeylmans van Emmichoven's reuniting of the Dutch National Society with the General Anthroposophical Society and with the Goetheanum at Easter 1960, after a 25-year period of separation. In the official letter that he wrote in honour of this event in September 1959, we find the following words: 'If we are now ready to become part of the General Society, this happens for the reason that we are of the opinion that time presses and that we would like to offer at least our contribution to building up the Anthroposophical Society, which can justify the name "general" through the fact that it includes all who feel themselves to be sincere pupils of Rudolf Steiner.'[36] Especially the concluding words of this extract have a great deal in common with the content of Marie Steiner's 'An Appeal for Reconciliation'. As for the question why he took this decision, Zeylmans van Emmichoven answered simply: 'Because we want to.' And later, in a private conversation, he added: 'to please Rudolf Steiner!'[37]

In Germany too, especially after the end of the Second World War, such prominent anthroposophists as Emil Bock, Fritz Götte, Clara and Rudolf Kreutzer and others were also working along the lines of such a fulfilment of Rudolf Steiner's central impulse. The efforts of the last two in particular were responsible for the arising in 1956 of the so-called 'Scheveninger Circle', which represented an important step on the path towards a gradual new consolidation of the Anthroposophical Society around the Goetheanum in Dornach.[38]

★

The significance of the *impulse of forgiveness* in Rudolf Steiner's life as we have described it has its deeper foundation in that the new path of initiation that was revealed by him to all mankind, as it is set forth in *Knowledge of the Higher Worlds* and *Occult Science*, is at the same time the modern form of that path of initiation which originated in the central figure of Christian esotericism, who in the fourteenth century bore the name of Christian Rosenkreutz.[39] Thus in the life of Rudolf Steiner—who from his youth was a direct pupil of Christian Rosenkreutz, and later in his books and lectures indicated on more than one occasion that the path of spiritual development outlined in them was at the same time his own spiritual path—we can find much of what is most characteristic of the all-embracing mission of his teacher. And the impulse of forgiveness is also one of its characteristic features.

The following words of Rudolf Steiner, which refer to the principal mission of Christian Rosenkreutz in the present and the future, can help us to understand the significance of the impulse of forgiveness in the life of this leading master of esoteric Christianity: 'Those who have any knowledge of this individuality know, too, that Christian Rosenkreutz will be the greatest martyr among human beings—apart from the Christ who suffered as a God. The sorrows that will lead him to become a great martyr will be caused by the fact that so few make the resolve to look into their own soul in order there to seek the evolving individuality, and to submit to the uncomfortable fact that truth will not be offered to one ready-made on a plate, but has to be acquired by intense struggle and effort—nothing else can be asked for in the name of him who is known as Christian Rosenkreutz.'[40]

As one familiarizes oneself with these striking words, it is first of all necessary to ask oneself: from whence will spring this great suffering of Christian Rosenkreutz in the future evolution of humanity? Its principal source will be the unwillingness of human beings independently to strive out of their own individuality, their own ego, towards a search for spiritual truth, and also their unwillingness to take upon themselves the responsibility for their own higher development. One could say that in a certain sense Christian Rosenkreutz will in future—which, however, is beginning already in our time—voluntarily take upon himself part of the karma of the evolving individual ego. And inasmuch as, in the present epoch of the rulership of materialism, mankind as a whole will be least of all inclined towards inner independence or towards such an individual search for spiritual truth but will, on the contrary, tend more towards complete inner passivity with respect to true spiritual knowledge, this karmic task which Christian Rosenkreutz has voluntarily taken upon himself will become for him a source of the greatest suffering. This suffering will be especially great because, once having taken on this task, Christian Rosenkreutz will, in accordance with the laws of the spiritual world, be unable to give it up until his mission has reached its fulfilment.

In other words, Christian Rosenkreutz has made a decision to *remain with humanity* and to serve as its spiritual leader, with absolute respect for the freedom of every individual and at the same time agreeing to take upon himself and to bear all the consequences of any possible misuse of it on the part of human beings such as result from their unwillingness truly to embark upon a path of individual spiritual development. However, it has remained possible for Christian Rosenkreutz to continue to be with humanity under such conditions—until such time as human beings finally awaken to individual inner activity—only by dint of a continual spiritual act of *higher forgiveness* with respect to all those many people who in our time for the most part have a fear of—and therefore have no intention of manifesting—even the slightest inner activity in the sense of the above words of Rudolf Steiner.[41]

From an occult point of view, such people can be responded to in one of two ways. One can either spiritually withdraw from them, which when regarded from a higher standpoint is equivalent to not forgiving them for such a conscious, or more often an unconscious, opposition to the true path of human evolution; or one can *forgive* them for this, thus enabling one spiritually to remain with them and, continuing to forgive them again and again, patiently to wait until through their inner freedom they have gained an awareness of the absolute necessity for the entire future evolution of individual spiritual initiative—a quality which is the basic precondition for Christian Rosenkreutz to number them among his pupils.

★

Here we have an image of that Way of the Cross that Christian Rosenkreutz now follows and which with the Christmas Conference Rudolf Steiner has also entered upon. Thus when asked about his relationship to Christian Rosenkreutz, Rudolf Steiner replied with an imagination in which at an altar in the spiritual world there stand, on the left of the altar, Christian Rosenkreutz in a blue stole and, on the right, Rudolf Steiner in a red stole.[42]

In this sense both teachers of esoteric Christianity stand in a spiritual respect beside one another and both are the direct successors and imitators of the divine Being of the Christ. For in the three years of His earthly life and His sufferings on the Cross, a higher archetype was given to all mankind of that path of *all-encompassing forgiveness* which Christian Rosenkreutz and Rudolf Steiner also follow.

This higher archetype finds its expression in the parting words of Christ Jesus, which He spoke from the Cross on Golgotha: 'Father, forgive them; for they know not what they do' (Luke 23:34). Since that time every individual who has attained true Christian initiation and who, as a result of this, is striving with his whole being, with all the forces of his soul, towards an imitation of Christ[43] will sooner or later inevitably have to embark upon this thorny path on which—in the wake of Christian Rosenkreutz and Rudolf Steiner—he will be called to become 'the greatest martyr among human beings' and at the same time one who is truly filled with boundless *forces of forgiveness*, for in a spiritual respect the one is inseparable from the other. Christian Rosenkreutz and the spiritual teachers connected with him, together with their initiated pupils, will bear this heavy cross of suffering and forgiveness for as long as there are people in the world 'who know not what they do' and who therefore have a continued need for higher forgiveness and who will need it until, finally, their eyes are opened for a 'knowledge' of the true realities of the spiritual world; this will come about only as part of a process of an ever greater development of a spiritually orientated inner activity of their souls.

★

If we consider as a whole the *seven* examples of forgiveness in this chapter, examples which give expression to the problem of forgiveness in its most diverse aspects from modern times to its most sublime archetype, we find that we have in the case of the last, in the words that sounded from the Cross about forgiving humanity as a whole, and each individual human being in past, present and future, an indication of the fundamental mystery of forgiveness, which has to do with its connection with the sphere of knowledge.

In this sense the *essential nature of forgiveness as a problem of knowledge* is not only one of the most vital questions of our time but also the most important problem which Anthroposophy, the modern science of the spirit, has to deal with. For only such a science of the spirit, resting as it does upon the results of supersensible research, is in our time really capable of resolving it in a manner that can satisfy the consciousness of today.

IV

The Nature of Forgiveness from a
Spiritual-Scientific Viewpoint

A consideration of the nature of forgiveness from a spiritual-scientific viewpoint may best begin with the characterization of the members of man's being which appears in the second chapter of Rudolf Steiner's book *Occult Science*. This characterization runs as follows: 'Forgetting is for the astral body what death is for the physical body and sleep for the etheric. Or, as we may also express it: life is proper to the etheric body, consciousness to the astral body, and memory to the ego.'[44]

We may understand these words of Rudolf Steiner in the following way. Man's physical body becomes a corpse the moment that the higher members of his being depart from it. Processes then take place in it which we encounter everywhere in the mineral world. Mineral substance as such is devoid of life. Life enters into it with the etheric body, as is the case with plants. But while plants have life they do not as yet possess consciousness, at any rate not in forms that are familiar to ordinary people. In its unconsciousness the plant is so to speak continually immersed in a deep sleep, like the dreamless sleep of a human being.

Awakening takes place only at the next, higher stage of natural existence, through the astral body, the bearer of consciousness, becoming united with the etheric body. An inner structure of this kind, one that contains the initial elements of consciousness, is possessed by animals. Thus in their life we find, for example, a constant rhythmical interplay between two states of consciousness—sleep and wakefulness, although both these conditions have marked differences with the human condition which they resemble. For the 'waking' state of an animal, which is called forth by the presence within it of the astral body, can really only be likened to dream consciousness in man, inasmuch as the consciousness of the astral body can out of itself attain only to the degree of clarity of a dream.

However, what an animal—that is, the astral body that works within it—altogether lacks is a consecutive unbroken stream of memory and the individual *self*-consciousness that is founded upon it. Only man, who in addition to having an astral body is also the bearer of an individual ego, possesses such self-consciousness. Hence Rudolf Steiner says of this connection between the astral body and the ego that '... the astral body would ever and again have to let the past sink into oblivion if the ego did not preserve the past and carry it over into the present.'[45]

Only in certain conditions of sickness can it happen that, when a person awakes from sleep, his dream consciousness—which has its source in the astral body—is sufficiently enveloped and irradiated by the influence of the outer impressions provided by the senses. There then takes place an unwarranted 'bubbling-over' of the astral body and the partial inundation by its forces, and above all by the lower dream-imbued will that lives within it, of the inner sphere of activity of man's waking ego-consciousness. Whereupon the astral body, in a seemingly wilful way, interrupts the unbroken stream of memory which constantly permeates and bears the ego, as a result of which man's clear, waking consciousness is supplanted by another kind of consciousness, the dim, lowered consciousness of the astral body which is comparable only with an experience of dreaming while one is awake.

In his lectures, Rudolf Steiner on several occasions gives an example to elucidate this process which, drawn from his own life, offers a particularly clear impression of it. In his youth he knew a certain person who all of a sudden lost his memory. When he got up in the morning, without being in the least aware of what was going on, he left his family and his home, got into a train and went away to a completely different town. There he again bought a ticket and travelled to a second town, from there to a third and so on. He journeyed like this for several weeks throughout Europe, without having the slightest idea of what he was actually doing. The consciousness of his astral body, together with the habits that had been inculcated within it by the earlier activity of his ego, continued outwardly to behave completely 'reasonably'—it bought tickets, looked at train timetables, observed all the rules of travelling on the railway, and so on, but his self-consciousness, that is, the consciousness of his ego, was not present in this. And all this continued until finally the continuity of his individual memory returned to him and he was aware of being in a completely strange town, in a doss-house for vagrants.[46]

Rudolf Steiner then goes on to make the following observation about this event from a spiritual-scientific standpoint: 'In a sense, we bear our memories with us as the treasure won from our experiences [in the outer world]. And if in certain pathological cases—of which I have already spoken—a part of these memories should be lost, it is due to the ego suffering injury.'[47] From this the absolute unwarrantability of such an influence of the astral body upon the ego, when—as a lower member of man's being—it illicitly encroaches upon the sphere of a higher member, thus undermining its rightful activity, becomes fully clear.★

After familiarizing ourselves with these preparatory thoughts, we can now begin to consider this process of forgiveness from the standpoint of modern spiritual science. For in the act of forgiveness we also call forth within us—though in full consciousness and through our own will—a kind of 'interruption' or moment of 'oblivion' in the unbroken stream of memory that is the foundation of our waking ego-consciousness. The only difference between an act of forgiveness, of *consciously* evoked oblivion, and the event cited above is that in the former case the individual human ego does not suffer the least degree of harm. On the contrary, its forces are, as a result, significantly strengthened, and man's inner world is purified and becomes far more spiritual. From this it follows that the spiritual power that is manifested in every act of true forgiveness, which by its very nature can only fortify the human ego, could not spring from the astral body which works upon the ego in a merely negative

★ More will be said in chapter VI, section 4, about the positive aspect of 'oblivion'/'forgetfulness' that is spoken of in *Occult Science* and in the lecture of 2 November 1908 (*The Being of Man and his Future Evolution*).

manner such as serves to darken its consciousness.

But what can influence the ego in a positive way? The fundamental pedagogical law formulated by Rudolf Steiner in the second lecture of the curative education course[48] offers us an answer to this question. In essence this states that a positive influence of one member of man's being upon another can be exerted only from a higher member to a lower, though never the other way round. Thus, for example, if a teacher wants to bring about a positive change in the physical body of his pupil or of someone entrusted to his care, he must influence it out of the forces of his etheric body. In order to have a positive influence upon the etheric body of his pupil or charge, the forces of his astral body are needed, and for a positive influence upon the astral body the forces of his ego. And then, finally, Rudolf Steiner formulates the next stage, the one that pertains to our question, as follows: '... an ego can be influenced only by what is living in a Spirit Self.' It should be added that this law is in itself only an earthly reflection of the mutual activity in the spiritual worlds of *all* the rightly evolved Hierarchies up to the very highest, both with one another and in their relation to man.

And so only man's higher ego or Spirit Self is able to influence the ordinary human ego in a positive sense, for it alone has the capacity not merely to avoid causing this latter member any injury but also to further its subsequent growth and evolution. Here we have an indication of the innermost nature of the *process of forgiveness*, namely, that man is able truly to forgive, that is, voluntarily and without the least injury to himself to interrupt the stream of memory that bears his individual ego, only if he allows the light of his higher ego to shine within the ordinary ego; or in other words, if he is enabled to permeate it with the forces of the Spirit Self. This means that the whole relationship of the higher and lower ego within man is rooted in the problem of forgiveness as such, so that without entering wholly into the nature and significance of forgiveness it is simply impossible to understand this relationship to the fullest extent. For what man's higher ego accomplishes with regard to his lower ego throughout earthly life can be expressed in human words as a *continual process of forgiveness*, forgiveness for all those countless mistakes and errors which the lower ego goes on making, largely because in an overwhelming majority of cases it is in a position of complete or partial ignorance (oblivion) with respect to the real impulses of the higher ego which constantly guides it.

If at this point we recall Rudolf Steiner's indication that the higher ego (Spirit Self) of every human being in the present cycle of his development is borne in the spiritual worlds by his Guardian Angel, and that therefore from a certain point of view it does not make any significant difference whether we say that the Spirit Self or his Angel is working within him,[49] what we have just said can also shed some light on the *essential nature* of a person's relationship with the Angel who guides and protects him. For all the relationships that an Angel has with the human being whom he guides are in the strictest accordance with the words of Christ cited above: 'Father, forgive them; for they know not what they do.' It is generally the case that, in his ordinary everyday consciousness, an individual knows virtually nothing about those intentions, those important decisions, that ideal plan for his future life on Earth which he has himself resolved upon and elaborated under the guidance of his Angel in his higher ego before his birth on the Earth. But as he does not know or have any recollection of this, he then carries out actions in his life and cherishes thoughts and feelings in his soul which are for the most part completely at odds with it. On the other hand, however, it is precisely this lack of awareness (one could also call it oblivion) which is the foundation of those almost infinite forces of forgiveness which the Angel constantly brings towards the human being whom he is guiding; because without these forces, that is, without his capacity to forgive again and again, or, in the words of Christ Jesus Himself, 'seventy times seven',* he would

---

* Matthew 18:22. The number given here refers to seven successive human incarnations, each of 70 years in length (70 years is the age of a patriarch, that is, of a single human life from an occult point of view). By the end of such a series of seven incarnations a person must have fully atoned for all the errors and karmic debts with respect to other people perpetrated or incurred at its beginning, so that by the 'eighth' incarnation he must be completely free from all the omissions and inadequacies of the 'first' and so on. If these karmic debts and these consequences of the wrongs which have been committed are not made good during the seven incarnations, difficulties will inevitably arise between the human individual and the Angel who guides him, which will prevent the latter from leading him further.

never be able rightly to lead the human being entrusted to him from incarnation to incarnation, to lead him without abandoning him even for a moment.

Thus a human individual is led by his Angel through earthly lives and through the periods of his life after death as part of the Angel's unceasing service to the Christ Being, whose impulse Angels who followed a rightful path of evolution took upon themselves earlier than human beings, during Christ's passage through the sphere of the Angels on His path towards incarnating on Earth in Jesus of Nazareth.[50]

★

From such a characterization of forgiveness, as an expression of the relationship between the higher and lower ego, it becomes possible to understand the connection (described in the previous chapter) of a leading initiate of Christian esotericism—such as Christian Rosenkreutz—to the higher ego of an individual human being. For the nature of this connection resembles that which a person's Guardian Angel has to him, inasmuch as the great initiates of humanity are already now anticipating in their development that condition which other human beings will attain only on Jupiter.

In the lecture of 18 October 1905 Rudolf Steiner characterizes such a relationship of an initiate to the higher ego of another human being in the following words: 'The higher self is something which lives not in us but around us. More highly developed individualities are the higher self. A human being must be quite clear that the higher self is outside him. If he were to seek it within, he would never find it. He must seek it among those who have already walked the path that we want to take ... If we would become really familiar with the higher self, we must search for it where it already is today—among the higher individualities. That is the intercourse of pupils with the masters.'[51]

If we read the numerous memoirs of Rudolf Steiner's personal pupils we may sense, through some of the descriptions, the impression which he made on them in one or another situation that the meeting with him represented the first meeting with their own higher ego—that they experienced it for the first time in their lives thanks to Rudolf Steiner.

To the extent to which the great initiates represent this higher ego among mankind, so must they continually fulfil those obligations which this latter member fulfils with respect to the lower ego, namely, continually forgiving it, in order to have the possibility of continuing to remain with it, helping it to move forward on the path of ascending, rather than descending, evolution. True initiates act in exactly the same way in their relationship to humanity.

If we bring all that has been said in this chapter into a single focus, we may say that the occult 'mechanism' of forgiveness is as follows. As a result of the effort of moral will that an act of forgiveness—that is, the conscious forgetting★ of an evil or injustice to which we have been subjected—evokes from the individual ego, there forms, so to speak, within the unbroken stream of memory which permeates our ego and bears our ego-consciousness, a 'space devoid of memory' into which the substance of the higher ego or Spirit Self, that is, the force which transforms all evil, can then flow. This substance of the Spirit Self, which is borne onwards by the stream of memory, penetrates through its mediation into the human ego, spiritualizing it ever more and more. As a result there arises not a narrowing but, on the contrary, an ever greater widening of ego-consciousness and at the same time its permeation by higher moral forces which bring it ever closer to an experience of its archetype, to an encounter with the Christ in the spiritual world nearest to the Earth.

★ What is meant here is not an ordinary kind of forgetting but rather that in this process all subjective reactions, such as inner protest or antipathy, must give way to perfect equanimity and acceptance of destiny. The injustice that has been inflicted can be wholly objectified by the person concerned and completely separated from his own personality. The negative, begrudging memory must gradually go through a kind of death (forgetting) in order to rise as *forgiveness*, that is, as a strong will to restore to the world the good of which it has been deprived by the wrongful deed. One will then remember such a deed only to the extent that this is necessary for true forgiveness to come about.

V

Forgiveness as an Essential Part of the Modern Path to Christ

The revelations of Christ will become manifest at ever higher levels.
That is the mystery of the evolution of Christ.
                                    Rudolf Steiner (lecture of 17 June 1910)

1. First Stage

At the beginning of our present study (chapter I), we spoke of how forgiveness is in itself merely a part of that particular path of spiritual development which is able to lead modern man to a real experience of the Christ and at the same time to a total transformation of his being.

This path consists initially of four stages. The first of these is essentially prior to the act of forgiveness as such, though it nevertheless plays a considerable part in our lives. This first stage consists in the development of genuine tolerance and can also be characterized as a kind of 'forgiveness on a small scale'.

We shall now attempt to examine this inner quality from a spiritual-scientific point of view. For this we must above all take the following into consideration. As we know through spiritual science, we are to a significant extent bound to the physical body by our waking *ego-consciousness*, or to be more exact by the impressions of the outer world which enter into us through our senses. One could say that the human ego, working from within, is continually running up against them and is thereby led again and again to an *awareness* of its own nature. This is manifested in a particularly striking way at the moment of awakening from sleep. As a rule, it is in this case the impressions of the outer world, entering into us through the gates of our senses, which bring about the act of awakening—the flaring up within us of our waking ego-consciousness.

And so from a certain point of view, the act of awakening takes place as a result of the interaction between the human ego and the physical body and, in particular, its sense-organs. Something similar, although in a different form, comes about with the development of real tolerance. Here, too, the central role is played by the inter-relationship between the human ego and the sense-organs. One simple example will serve to clarify this.

Let us imagine that there is someone whom we do not like. It may be that when we are next to him we experience that his very presence irritates us through the whole spectrum of our sense-organs. We may be irritated by the way he looks, by how he behaves, thinks and moves—in other words, all his attributes, including the timbre of his voice and the smell of his breath, may appear to us to be quite repulsive. In the course of a more subtle, discriminating observation it may even emerge that these irritating influences of his, those which we experience as 'negative', can enter into our ego through practically *all* twelve senses, especially through the seven which are directed more towards the outer world (the senses of ego, thought and word; the senses of hearing, warmth, sight and taste).[52]

Such a state of affairs has its foundation in that at the present period of the earthly evolution of the human ego, which is still under the powerful influence of the unenlightened astral body, the outer sense-organs are used in such a way that they more readily convey to the ego information about the negative qualities of a particular being or event in the outer world. This is the source of that general intolerance which is so widespread in modern civilization and which must quite definitely be overcome on the path that we have delineated. But how can it be overcome? What is needed above all is a completely new education of the senses themselves. And if a person has not had the good fortune in youth to receive such an education in a Waldorf School, in his family, or in some other way, he can and must compensate for this lack, later in life, with the help of the conscious efforts of his ego. Thus in his maturer years his own ego must become the educator of his senses, successively training them to perceive in every being and process of the outer world, in the first instance, its positive side and quality. And if one really wants to, one can find such aspects in *every* process, event or being. This is, however, only possible through developing an intense *moral thinking*, for it alone is capable of becoming that instrument which our ego needs if it is gradually to re-educate our senses in the manner indicated.

In his articles on the 'Michael Mystery', Rudolf Steiner referred in the following words to the inner character of such a moral thinking: 'he [man] indeed thinks with his head, but his heart feels the radiance or shadowiness of a thought.'[53] Intense thinking activity that is directed towards the moral transformation of thinking and its purification from any element of egoism or self-love can gradually make of it the best 'teacher' of our sense-organs in perceiving primarily the *positive* aspects of all the events and beings in the outer world; this, in turn, may serve as a firm foundation for the development of true tolerance.

In his book *Knowledge of the Higher Worlds*, Rudolf Steiner referred to this essential precondition of the soul for spirit-pupilship in the following words: 'If I encounter a human being and blame him for his weaknesses, I rob myself of the power of higher knowledge; but if I try to enter lovingly into his qualities, I master this power. The pupil must bear this advice constantly in mind. Experienced spiritual investigators know how much power they owe to the circumstances that ever and again they look for the good in all things and withhold critical judgement.'[54]

Perhaps the most powerful spiritual-pedagogical and at the same time artistic example of this is the sculptural Group carved by Rudolf Steiner for the First Goetheanum, depicting Christ as the Representative of Humanity between Lucifer and Ahriman. When one contemplates it, one may experience the following. At first one's gaze is, in an apparently quite natural way, wholly drawn by the central figure. This impression of a *direct encounter* can attain such a power and intensity that as one beholds it one does not at first see anything other than the Representative of Humanity in front of one. Only after some time has gone by, when this first all-absorbing impression is increasingly enveloped with consciousness, it seems as though two streams open up before one's eyes, streams which issue from the heart region of the central figure in the direction of its arms, one extended upwards and the other down-wards; and only as one follows these streams does one gradually notice the presence of the beings of opposition around the Representative of Humanity.

Thus as we contemplate the Group solely by trying to be aware of its artistic and spiritual influence, there is revealed to us first the central Mystery of good and only then the Mystery of the dual aspect of evil. In other words, our gaze is at first naturally directed towards what is objectively good in the world and in man, and only after this—when our soul has already been strengthened by it—towards the evil, for its subsequent transformation by good into a new positive force. On the other hand, if we were to begin from the perception of evil in a particular being or object without having first strengthened the soul by searching for its good sides, that is, without detecting in it the working and the presence of the Christ forces, we might—although we might not perhaps even be aware of this at first—become too easily inwardly ensnared by the evil powers. These latter forces therefore try to show us in the surrounding world only what is related to evil, and which would make it impossible for us to find in outer events and beings the good that is hidden within them.

Thus in the sculptural Group, a modern clairvoyant conscious-ness has given us not only a remarkable work of art but also a highly important *educative* tool, which is able to awaken within man the deepest forces of tolerance and, hence, enable him to enter upon the path which is spoken of in this chapter.

This path begins with the development of a real *interest* in the other person, which is possible only if one's attention is consistently directed towards the positive qualities of good that live within him. Only such an interest, which can be manifested through all twelve senses, can then lead to the arising of a truly all-embracing *tolerance*, which Rudolf Steiner characterizes for our time as 'the way to the

Christ through thinking.'[55] And in the same lecture he designates the inner call, which resounds in the world for every spiritually open ear to forgive again and again—even in the smallest things—the human being who stands beside us, as one which issues directly from the Etheric Christ Himself: 'And thus He speaks today to those who want to hear: "In whatever the least of your brethren thinks, you must recognize that I am thinking in him, and that my feeling is united with yours whenever you bring another's thought into relation with your own, whenever you feel a fraternal interest for what is going on in the other person's soul. Whatever opinion, whatever outlook on life you discover in the least of your brethren, therein you are seeking Myself." So does the Christ speak to our life of thought, He who wills to reveal Himself in a new way—the time for it is approaching—to the people of the twentieth century.'[56] And then Rudolf Steiner goes on to clarify this: 'We shall not find Him [the Christ] if we remain egoistically bound up with our own thoughts, but only if we relate our own thoughts to those of other people, if we expand our *interest* into an inner *tolerance* for everything human ...'

Thus the gradual educating of our senses, beginning with the 'sense of ego', the 'sense of thought' and then including all the other senses, and leading to the gradual achievement of a real *tolerance* with respect to all manifestations of the individual ego, ways of thinking and all other aspects of human nature, especially in social life—this the Etheric Christ, in His new revelation, is calling upon mankind to achieve in our present age.* This is the concrete manifestation in our age of the deep spiritual-scientific truth that 'the Christ-impulse lies directly on the line of an evolving thinking.'[57]

All that we have said so far can be summarized in the following diagram:

---

* Many people who approached Rudolf Steiner for advice with regard to their inner development or some difficulty in their lives experienced such a tolerance and higher interest, embracing their whole being (that is, through all twelve senses). Every visitor felt himself to be fully accepted and understood, not merely in all his inadequacies and weaknesses but also in all his aspirations and spiritual striving.

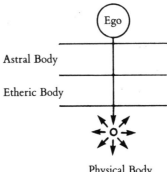

Physical Body

2. Second Stage

Turning now to the second stage of this path, we again approach the principal theme of the present work—the essential nature of forgiveness. For in a certain sense true forgiveness is nothing other than a higher, one could also say potentized, act of tolerance. In this sense both stages are connected as aspects of the moral transformation of the personality that is seeking a new knowledge and a new experience of the Christ Being.

As has already been shown in the previous chapter, a true act of forgiveness (more will be said later about its distinguishing features) is impossible without at least a partial permeation of the earthly human ego with the substance of its higher ego or Spirit Self. However, just as at the first stage the human ego is—through moral thinking—able to purify the senses and educate them towards perceiving primarily all that is good and beautiful in the world, so at the second stage the Spirit Self is—as it permeates the human ego—able from within to strengthen and inspire it to such an extent that it may in time become possible for it to perceive the world not only with the physical senses but also with the higher organs of perception of the etheric body. In other words, exactly as man's earthly ego needs the sense-organs of the physical body—which are formed in it from without during the period of embryological development—for his conscious state of existence, so does the Spirit Self need the perceptive organs of the etheric body for its conscious existence within man. It begins to form these within it the moment that it has entered into the earthly ego. As the Spirit Self permeates the earthly ego in the act of forgiveness, it can at the same time become the 'educator', though now of the etheric body, bringing about within it the gradual dissolution of all those 'callouses' and 'clots of darkness' which continually arise as an ultimate consequence of our earthly errors, the moral inadequacies of our character, untruthful thoughts and, especially, rancour and envy. In a spiritual sense, envy is one of the forms of rancour.

We know from numerous descriptions by Rudolf Steiner that in all processes of remembering and forgetting the etheric body plays a decisive part. Thus at the moment of forgiveness, when under the influence of our higher ego we consciously 'blot out' from our memory all the consequences of the wrong that has been perpetrated against us, we thereby at the same time liberate our etheric body from all its destructive and darkening elements. As we dissolve them in an act of forgiveness through the power of the Spirit Self, we make our etheric body more and more radiant and transparent and, in the course of further purification, also *visible* in the elemental (astral) world that surrounds it. For a sufficiently long activity on the part of the Spirit Self within our ego eventually renders it perceptible to outward impressions not only through the physical but also through the etheric or life body. We can illustrate what has been said here by means of the following diagram:

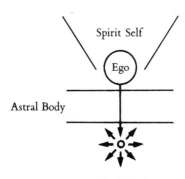

Etheric Body

What is revealed to man in the first instance clairvoyantly—through the awakened organs of perception of his etheric body—is a direct contemplation of the Etheric Christ in the spiritual world nearest to the Earth. Thus Rudolf Steiner refers to the direct connection that in our time begins to exist between the gradual entry into human consciousness of the forces of the Spirit Self (though the culmination of this process will be reached only in the following sixth cultural epoch) and the supersensible perception of the Etheric Christ: 'But we must be clear that we are now . . . gradually working from life in the consciousness soul to life in the Spirit Self. I have frequently pointed out in what way the entry into the Spirit Self is manifested. I have pointed out that the people who will experience the appearance of the Christ-impulse in the coming three thousand years will become ever greater in number, that human beings will gradually become capable of experiencing the Christ-impulse in the spiritual worlds.'[58]

Depending upon a person's individual disposition, his karma, and the actual circumstances of his life, this process of the influence of an ego—that has been strengthened by the Spirit Self—upon the etheric body may lead at first not to the forming of the supersensible organs of perception which are an essential prerequisite for the awakening within it of new clairvoyant faculties but to its inner transformation in a somewhat different direction, namely, making it particularly receptive to perceiving the macrocosmic forces of the universal etheric life. In a particular case it may even happen that, with an individual who has in the act of forgiveness achieved a considerable purification of his etheric body, there at first develops not an etheric clairvoyance but, so to speak, its *opposite*—that is, not a supersensible contemplation of Christ but a heightened receptivity to a perception of the macrocosmic life-forces that issue from Him. As a result of this, although the individual himself is not as yet beholding Christ clairvoyantly, nevertheless He is indeed working within his etheric body—and the other people around him may under certain conditions experience His direct presence *through such a person*—while the individual himself gains access to the truly inexhaustible sources of cosmic life.

We encounter such a phenomenon as this in the figure of Bill

Cody as described in George Ritchie's book. Herein lies the explanation of his remarkable physical and soul forces, which were nourished by the actual presence of the forces of the Christ in his etheric body, and also of the fact that other people were able to experience *through him* a meeting with the Etheric Christ, as was vouchsafed to George Ritchie himself. Thus from this example it follows with particular clarity that for our time the *path of forgiveness* is the most direct and surest path whereby the spiritual forces of the Etheric Christ may flow into modern earthly civilization, while the person himself is sooner or later enabled to gain a clairvoyant experience of Him.

All that has just been said enables us to come closer to the riddle of the fundamental problem of Simon Wiesenthal, that problem which was placed before him at the bedside of the dying SS man and which then pursued him throughout his life. For Simon Wiesenthal's question as to whether or not he should forgive this grave crime that had been committed (and so deeply repented by the youth) is merely the outward expression of the central problem of every modern human being, the problem of Christ. To forgive in that most difficult of life situations in which Simon Wiesenthal found himself would have meant approaching a direct experience of the Etheric Christ, while not to forgive would have signified turning away from Him. Simon Wiesenthal chose neither the one nor the other. He heard the dying man's confession to the end and only after this quietly left the room without saying a word, and so he allowed the question to remain open. However, the very fact that the irresolvable nature of this question, and his doubts therein, tormented him to such an extent for many long years, and finally compelled him to write a whole book, testifies to the feeling that was never to leave him—though perhaps it had never fully penetrated his consciousness—that at the bedside of the repentent criminal he missed the greatest opportunity of his entire life, the opportunity of a meeting with Him who was invisibly present, as a *Third*, in that military hospital in Lemberg. And while this meeting could not at that time have taken place, the fact that this problem continued to torment Simon Wiesenthal throughout his subsequent life speaks of how, in the inner struggle for its resolution, seeds were sown in his soul which sooner or later—in this life or in the life after death—will spring forth for his awakening spiritual consciousness as a question, as a longing for Christ!

3. Third Stage

As we turn to a consideration of the further steps of the path that we are describing, it should be observed that, while the second of these steps can in principle be taken by *everyone*, the two that follow no longer relate to the general development of contemporary humanity but to the path of initiation which leads beyond its bounds.[59] However, in setting out further on this path as a pupil of the spirit, it is possible for every human being of modern times, albeit only by way of making a small beginning, to embark upon the work that leads to the attainment of this third stage as well.

The initial effort will consist in developing a heightened sense of responsibility for the actions of a fellow human being, a community, a people or even the whole of humanity. Such an extended responsibility for everything that takes place in the world, accepted and borne by a person in freedom, can do much to prepare him, even in ordinary life, for the third stage of this path.

Now it is no longer simply a question of forgiveness but of *consciously taking upon oneself the karma of another person* * or even of a group of people. The spirit-pupil, and to an even greater extent the modern initiate, is able to achieve this as a result of the more extensive powers of his ego. This is only possible through permeating it not only with the principle of the Spirit Self but with a yet higher principle of the spiritual being of man—his Life Spirit. In Eastern terminology the Life Spirit is also called the principle of Buddhi or the all-embracing cosmic principle of love. In this sense the 'cosmic Buddhi' can be called the Christ,[60] who brought to the Earth the substance of cosmic love and then, in order that the whole

* The process of becoming united with the karma of another person, albeit only in its earliest stages, begins—as will be shown below—with an act of true forgiveness.

of earthly evolution might be permeated by it, took upon Himself the karma of all mankind at the Mystery of Golgotha.

At this stage too, the spirit pupil tries to follow this central archetype of earthly evolution, working upon the conscious development not only of his Spirit Self but also of his Life Spirit, that is of that utterly selfless and fully spiritualized love for human beings which alone can give him the necessary forces for taking upon himself their karma.

And when Rudolf Steiner, after the Christmas Conference of 1923/24, speaks of the newly founded General Anthroposophical Society as a karmic community which has as its central task the transformation of the old and the creation of a new 'Michaelic' karma, he has in mind making a first step in this direction. For what in our time is as yet very difficult for an individual human being to achieve can be accomplished to a significantly greater degree by a society of spiritually striving men and women. The permeation of man with the substance of the Life Spirit has yet another highly important consequence. For when the individual ego is strengthened by the Life Spirit it can gradually form organs of supersensible perception not only in the etheric body but in the higher astral body. The following diagram may make this clear.

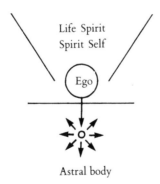

Astral body

As a result of this, man will eventually gain access to a new and even more all-embracing revelation of Christ, which Rudolf Steiner characterizes as His manifestation to the seer in the astral body on lower Devachan or in the lower regions of the Spirit-land, as distinct from His previous revelation in the etheric body on the astral plane or—which is the same thing—in the Soul-world.

Moreover, only this still more exalted experience of Christ can give man the strength not merely to take upon himself but also to *bear* into the future the karma of other people. For just as the Etheric Christ works in the act of forgiveness, so does the Cosmic (Astral) Christ work in every conscious or even unconscious act of taking upon oneself the karma of another person. One could also say that the receiving and bearing of another's karma is altogether impossible for man without at least a very rudimentary contact with this higher sphere of Christ's revelation.

4. Fourth Stage

Finally, the fourth and in a certain sense the highest stage is one where it is a matter not only of taking upon oneself the karma of another person or of a small group of people but of participating in the bearing of the karma of *the whole of humanity*. In the description given above (chapter III) of the great sufferings of Christian Rosenkreutz, we have a direct testimony of the attainment by him of precisely this stage of the path under consideration. For by continually *forgiving* humanity for all those torments which it is inflicting upon him in our time—and which it will to an ever-increasing degree in the future—he is thereby enabled to remain unfailingly with it, without abandoning it for a moment, in order through this to participate further in the bearing of the karma of the evolving individual ego, unceasingly following in this respect his divine teacher—Christ Himself.

From an occult point of view this fourth stage can be attained by the initiate only as a result of such a further development of the inner forces of his individual ego as may enable it to form for itself organs of higher supersensible perception directly out of its own substance, without any need for the mediatory activity of the three lower bodies or sheaths (the physical, etheric and astral bodies). This is possible for the ego of the initiate only when it can, even to a small degree, permeate itself not only with the substance of the

Spirit Self and the Life Spirit, as at the previous stages, but also with the substance of the *Spirit Man*:

Inner Sun of the Soul

The stage of inner development of the initiate that we have characterized gives him access to the next, third and, for the present cycle of evolution, the highest revelation of Christ, namely, His revelation on higher Devachan as the all-encompassing Ego of our cosmos. Only now does Christ appear before man directly in His innermost essence and without any of the veils which, as though 'deferring before' the imperfection of man's capacity for spiritual perception, He had to adopt at the lower planes of existence, manifesting Himself on the astral plane in an etheric garment and on lower Devachan in an astral garment. Now all these intervening sheaths fall away and the initiate is in a position to perceive Christ out of his own ego which has become clairvoyant—as his true cosmic archetype, as the cosmic, universal Ego.

What at the previous stages was a knowledge of the Christ Being gained by means of a transformed thinking, through what Rudolf Steiner calls 'intellectual clairvoyance', that is, a thinking that has been exalted to Imaginations which lead to a contemplation of the Etheric Christ;[61] and what was then revealed to a feeling that has been transmuted into a capacity for Inspirations, now culminates—through a total transformation of the human will—in an experience of Him in *Intuition*, as the cosmic Ego who is directly apprehended by the human ego and who at the same time permeates it, for such is the nature of intuitive knowledge.[62]

Rudolf Steiner speaks about this whole series of supersensible revelations of Christ, culminating in His higher ego-revelation, in the following words: 'So we see how, starting from a physical, earthly human entity, the Christ who has descended to the Earth gradually evolves as Etheric Christ, Astral Christ and Ego Christ, in order, as Ego Christ, to become the Spirit of the Earth who then rises to ever higher stages together with all mankind.'[63]

It has already been observed that the leading individuality of esoteric Christianity, Christian Rosenkreutz, and also some of his more advanced colleagues and pupils, are already at a stage of inner development such as enables them to participate in bearing the karma of the evolving ego of all mankind. This is inevitably associated with a willing acceptance of the considerable sufferings that are called forth by inner passivity and the numerous abuses of freedom to which people are now prone. In order to endure this suffering the initiate needs truly immense inner forces. These forces are derived by initiates from a constant contemplation of the third supersensible revelation of Christ, where He appears to them as the new Spirit Guardian or Ego of the Earth, who has taken upon Himself the karma of the whole of mankind.

5. The Redemption of the Opposing Forces

This stage of inner development opens up to the initiate one further highly important realm of activity. Having raised himself to this fourth stage, he can in a completely new way take part not only in the liberation and perfection of the human race but also in the gradual redemption of the opposing forces that have participated in earthly evolution, which in modern spiritual science are called the luciferic and the ahrimanic.

In former times, in the distant past of Earth evolution, these beings made a kind of sacrifice in taking the decision to distance themselves from the general evolution of beings similar to themselves, in order that, through continually having to resist them and in the course of overcoming the hindrances that they created, man might unfold within himself completely new forces and far higher capacities than would have been the case without such endeavours—most notably the capacity to experience inner freedom.[64] But there is another aspect to this participation of the opposing spirits in earthly evolution. It is that, through being separated from rightly evolved beings similar to themselves, they were forced to transfer the field of their activity to a different cosmic realm, whence any further evolution *on their own part* would be impossible. Reference is made to this occult fact in a more familiar form in the picture of the battle of the Archangel Michael with the dragon, whom he compels continually to remain down beneath his feet.

A further evolution for these beings is possible only through their being united with the central impulse of our cosmos, the Christ-impulse. But they are unable to achieve this out of themselves. The only way in which they can return to a path of rightful evolution is to gain access to the Christ-impulse where this is alone possible for them at present, namely, *within man*. This means that the potential for the redemption of the beings of opposition and their con-comitant future return to the bosom of general world evolution has to a certain extent been given over into the hands of human beings by the higher powers.

The process of their liberation will consist in that, as a result of a conscious process of inner evolution, man will be able to oppose every luciferic or ahrimanic influence in his soul with another influence, which proceeds directly from the Christ Being. Using the example of the luciferic beings, Rudolf Steiner describes this process in the following way: 'By effacing with, and only with, Christ's help all those human qualities which come from Lucifer, we as human beings also gradually liberate the luciferic powers. There will come a time when the luciferic powers—who in the course of Moon evolution had for the salvation of human freedom to sink down to a lower level of evolution and did not have the opportunity to experience the power of Christ on the Earth—will experience the Christ power, and will be redeemed, through human beings. Man will redeem Lucifer if he receives the power of Christ in the appropriate way.'[65]

The process of this gradual 'liberation' of the luciferic forces has been guided by the great initiates of mankind—whom Rudolf Steiner calls 'The Masters of Wisdom and of the Harmony of

Feelings'—for almost two thousand years, from the moment when the Mystery of Golgotha was fulfilled on the Earth. Since the fifteenth century, a second task was gradually added to the first, that of also 'redeeming' the ahrimanic beings. But while in our time *every* individual—albeit only in a small way—is able to participate in the 'liberation' of Lucifer through receiving the Christ-impulse into his soul, working towards the liberation of Ahriman, even in a small way, is possible only for a social community of human beings. To accomplish this on an individual basis is in our time possible only for the highest initiates.

Here it should be clearly stressed that one is speaking of redemption or liberation and not simply of driving the opposing beings from a particular sphere of activity within man. Such a thing was possible for individual people and, in particular, for strictly enclosed esoteric communities at all times, also before the Mystery of Golgotha. In the lectures on *The Fifth Gospel*, Rudolf Steiner demonstrates this with considerable power and vividness through the example of the order of the Essenes, at whose gates Jesus of Nazareth had a spiritual experience which was decisive for him: in the spirit he saw Lucifer and Ahriman fleeing from the order's precincts and then rushing *towards other people*, plunging them into ever greater calamities and subjecting them to yet further temptations.

On the other hand, their *redemption* presupposes above all a far deeper and more comprehensive *knowledge* of their natures, their places in our cosmos, and the whole character of their activity in the world and in man. For once this knowledge, which has its source in true Christian esotericism and is now imparted to all mankind in Anthroposophy, has been received into human consciousness, it will quite out of itself serve as the *beginning* of the process of redeeming these beings.

According to spiritual science, each of the aforementioned categories of opposing beings also has a rightful sphere of activity in our cosmos: Lucifer, for example, in the realm of 'the beauty of appearances', in fantasy and art; Ahriman, at that frontier where the forces of dead matter work, and also in the sphere of science and, most especially, technology. However, in these regions of their rightful activity the higher Gods have doomed them to a continual and unendurable suffering, which consists in the complete impossibility of any further evolution on their part. In a spiritual sense their situation could be compared with the medieval torture whereby a person was encased while still a child in a close-fitting suit of armour, and as he grew physically thereafter this only brought him more and more unendurable suffering. The words of Strader from the Third Mystery Play, *The Guardian of the Threshold*, spoken as he contemplates Ahriman in his kingdom, refer to this desperate situation of the opposing forces in their own realm:

> In your rough words sounds pain
> From you—in me too they are pain.
> Looking on you—I can but ... mourn, and weep.[66]

Continually experiencing unbearable sufferings in their own domain, the opposing powers seek any possibility of escaping from it, even for a moment, of finding some sort of relief. In other words, by all means available to them they make ceaseless attempts to cross the frontier of 'what is permitted', to cross the frontier of their own domain, as originally given to them by the higher Gods, everywhere encroaching upon human evolution and then working within it as tempters and as the spirits of every manner of hindrance. Here, delivered for a while from their sufferings, they appear either as unjustifiably proud or as super-intelligent beings, everywhere offering man their enticing 'gifts' but actually only bringing about destruction and ruin.[67]

Strader refers to this fact in the same scene as follows:

> But what is wrung here from my soul?
> The words I speak destroy me, if on Earth
> I were to find them true.

This means that *outside* Ahriman's kingdom, that is, in the sphere of human evolution itself, man is *obliged* to resist Ahriman—and the same is true for Lucifer—with all his forces, though not in the sense of pitting evil or violence against evil but through opposing it with true *goodness*. From an occult point of view this can be achieved only through consciously resisting the opposing spirits not by means of the weak forces of human beings but through man receiving the Christ-impulse into his being, so that every time that Lucifer and Ahriman try to go beyond the limits of their rightful activity within man by seeking to seduce him they would encounter in him the forces of the Christ. Then it will not be man himself but the Christ within him who will be able to turn Lucifer and Ahriman towards the good; in this lies the very essence of all true Manichaean Mysteries.

This entire process is portrayed in the north, peach-blossom coloured window of the First Goetheanum. In its central motif is depicted man's meeting with Christ in the etheric world nearest to the Earth and the receiving of His Being into himself. On the left and right [side] panels, the consequences of this act of receiving are shown: the redemption by Christ of Lucifer, who has remained behind on Old Moon; and His redemption of Ahriman, who has remained at a still earlier stage, on Old Sun. The symbols of Moon and Sun refer both to their origin and also to the astral (Moon) and etheric (Sun) bodies of man, into the first of which luciferic forces penetrated on ancient Lemuria and, into the second, ahrimanic forces on Atlantis.[68]

Only once having attained the fourth, and for the present the highest, stage of the path that we are considering and through having come to abide in the sphere of the third supersensible revelation of Christ, that is, experiencing His constant presence in his own ego in full consciousness as the real fulfilment of the words 'Not I, but Christ in me', can the modern initiate really become the liberator not only of the human race but also of the beings of opposition. For now, as they enter into such an initiate, the opposing beings will find Christ within him no longer in His etheric or astral sheaths but in His primal essence, as the all-encompassing Ego of our cosmos and at the same time as the new Guardian Spirit of the whole Earth.[69]

Thus what at previous stages was no more than a preliminary, quite rudimentary work towards liberating the opposing beings, which led to their being able to encounter Christ within man not directly, in His primal essence, but only through the mediation of His etheric and astral sheaths, now, from this stage onwards, begins as the conscious process of their complete and final redemption. Now, permeated by Christ, the ego of the initiate begins to shine like a Sun into the darkness of his outer sheaths, engendering 'light' in his astral body, 'life' in his etheric body and 'resurrection' in his physical body, that is, repeating on a microcosmic scale what is referred to in those first verses of St John's Gospel which tell of the macrocosmic descent of the Logos to mankind. One could also say that since this time the Christ-impulse, issuing from the human ego, has permeated his sheaths in such a way that the words 'Not I, but Christ in me' have come to fulfilment first in his astral body, then in his etheric body, and finally—in the perspective of future evolution—in his physical body.

The esoteric work of all leading Christian initiates who bear the Sun of Christ in their ego, those whom Rudolf Steiner called the 'Masters of Wisdom and of the Harmony of Feelings', lies in this direction. In concrete terms this means that, being permeated by its *light*, its astral light, they give Lucifer the opportunity to find redemption through coming into contact with it. Then, through permeating their etheric body with the *life* that streams from the Sun of Christ into their ego, they gradually make it possible for Ahriman to win redemption through a direct contact with it. Only in the most distant future, by fully permeating their physical bodies with the forces of *love* which proceed from the Christ Sun into their ego, will they also open up a path to the third category of opposing beings, the Asuras. This is, however, only the beginning of this work of redemption; its eventual fulfilment in earthly evolution will only come when the *whole* of humanity has risen to those levels at which the higher initiates of the Earth are living and working now. Thus in the perspective of world evolution as a whole it is not human beings themselves but the Christ in them (in the sense of the words 'Not I, but Christ in me') who will be the great liberator of all three categories of opposing spirits.

Expressing this more in the language of spiritual science, one could say that the process of redeeming Lucifer will consist in the permeation of man's astral body with Spirit Self forces that have been imbued by the Christ-impulse, the redemption of Ahriman through permeating the etheric body with Life Spirit forces that have been imbued by the Christ-impulse, and the future redemption of the Asuras through the permeation of man's physical body with Spirit Man forces that have been imbued by Christ, that is, by the forces of the 'Resurrection body' (Phantom).[70]

All the foregoing is most immediately connected with the incarnation, earthly life, death and Resurrection of the Sun Being of the Christ. For the possibility of working on the redeeming of the opposing beings was brought into earthly evolution through the three years of Christ's life on Earth and through the Mystery of Golgotha, as a result of which the fruits of this three-year life have entered into earthly evolution as a whole. Thus during the first year, through His cosmic Ego, Christ wholly transformed the astral body of Jesus of Nazareth into the Spirit Self; during the second year He wholly transformed his etheric body into the Life Spirit; and during the third year, which culminated in the Mystery of Golgotha, He fully transformed his physical body into Spirit Man, which then rose from the grave of Golgotha as the new Resurrection body (Phantom). By this means, the foundation was laid in Earth evolution for the subsequent liberation by human beings themselves— in so far as they strive to make the fruits of this three-year life of Christ an inner reality—of the luciferic, ahrimanic and asuric powers.

6. The Particular Significance of the Redemption of Lucifer in Our Time

In the line of development that we have outlined, the most important aspect for our time is the redemption of Lucifer. As a result of the work which has been done in this respect by the Masters of Wisdom and of the Harmony of Feelings throughout virtually the last two millennia, his redemption had progressed sufficiently far as to enable Rudolf Steiner at the beginning of our century to speak openly about this important occult mystery in his lectures, which he did most notably in the lecture given in Berlin on 22 March 1909.[71]

By enabling the light of the Christ Sun that is shining within their ego to pour forth into their astral body, such initiates create within themselves the conditions that are necessary for Lucifer to come into direct contact with it. This must inevitably lead to a situation whereby Lucifer, having come into contact with the light of Christ, will henceforth willingly become His servant, that is, the new bearer in the cosmos of His light, which is what in earliest times the name 'lucifer' or 'phosphorus' used to mean—the 'light-bearer'. Then, having turned his whole being towards Christ, he will have been transformed into a completely new being, into a being filled with the Holy Spirit. From then on, as the cosmic bearer of the light of the Christ Sun, he will, in his service to it, become the guide of every human individual who is striving towards higher knowledge, who is endeavouring to penetrate the most deeply hidden mysteries of the cosmos in connection with its central Mystery, the Mystery of the Christ.

In Christ's farewell discourses, as they have been recounted in the most esoteric of the four Gospels, that of St John, we have an indication of this mystery of the future redemption of Lucifer. There, Christ Himself speaks of the Paraclete or Spirit of Comfort who is to come (14:16). From an esoteric standpoint this is none other than a reference to the redeemed Lucifer who, as henceforth the servant of Christ, will have as his new task that of bringing to people at Christ's behest the renewed impulse of the Holy Spirit who will be able to reveal to them the true knowledge of Christ.[72]

From this it becomes easier to understand why the first cycle of lectures (of those that had been expressly given only for members of the Society) which Rudolf Steiner, in 1921, decided to publish quite openly in the magazine *Die Drei* was the cycle *The East in the Light of the West. The Children of Lucifer and the Brothers of Christ*— lectures which he had given twelve years before, in August 1909 in Munich, in connection with a production of Edouard Schuré's play, *The Children of Lucifer*. In this play the theme of Lucifer's redemption occupies a central position. At this same time and in the same cycle, a description was given of the sources of Christian-Rosicrucian esotericism, sources which go back to one of the most important spiritual councils in the Christian era, which took place in the fourth century. Four of the leading Masters of Wisdom and of the Harmony of Feelings, Manes, Scythianos, Zarathustra and Buddha, took part in this council, those who—with the later addition of Christian Rosenkreutz—have played and continue to play an essential part in the redemption of Lucifer. From this perspective a detailed plan for his redemption was drawn up by them at the council that has been referred to, whereby the wisdom of the Bodhisattvas that has its origin in the cosmic sphere of the Holy Spirit was in future to flow into the evolution of esoteric Rosicrucian Christianity on Earth, so that an ever deeper understanding of the Christ Being and the Mystery of Golgotha might emerge.[73]

Even the name of the journal that Rudolf Steiner published at the beginning of the century under the aegis of the Theosophical Society, *Lucifer-Gnosis,* acquires through this a deeper, occult significance. For through this journal, mankind was to be given a new cosmic knowledge of Christ, a knowledge that stemmed from a Lucifer who had turned to Christ and was henceforth serving Him as the new 'Light-bearer': 'The new-born Lucifer, Lucifer who has turned to the good, bearing aloft the torch for Christ. He bears the Christ Himself. He is the bearer of light, Christ is the light.'[74]

However, the fact that Rudolf Steiner revealed to anthroposophists this mystery of Lucifer's redemption, which had been held in trust hitherto only by the Masters of Wisdom and of the Harmony of Feelings and their closest pupils, also had a further and quite different significance. This is that, in the new age of light which began after the end of the dark age of the Kali Yuga in 1899, the conscious work on his further redemption must be carried out not only by initiates who are hidden from the world and by their esoteric pupils but also by all followers of modern spiritual science who are striving towards a true knowledge of Christ, not only as an earthly but above all as an all-encompassing cosmic Being: 'But man may, if he chooses, recognize Christ even now! Now is the time for him to gather together all the wisdom that he needs to recognize Christ. What does he do by this? Something quite considerable! When man recognizes Christ, when he really gains insight into the wisdom needed to perceive who Christ is, he liberates both himself and the luciferic beings through this knowledge of Christ.'[75]

When, on the other hand, he speaks about the future redemption

of Ahriman, Rudolf Steiner for the most part confines himself
merely to the most general indications—really no more than
hints.[76] For in the present epoch of evolution, only initiates who are
at the level of the Masters of Wisdom and of the Harmony of
Feelings, or at any rate close to it, can work in any real way upon the
redemption of Ahriman, while for the rest of humanity, on the
other hand, it is necessary to make every possible effort to resist all
forms of his unwarranted influence upon earthly evolution; this is
possible only through ever wider circles of present-day humanity
acquiring a real knowledge of Ahriman, of his nature, and of the
place and character of his activity in the world and in man. This will
be particularly necessary in view of his incarnation on Earth, which
is to come about at the beginning of the third millennium, and the
severe trials that this will bring with it for all mankind.[77]

As regards the third category of opposing spirits, not even the
Masters of Wisdom and of the Harmony of Feelings have fully
approached the task of their redemption, for the activity of these
most dangerous of beings, together with the temptations associated
with them, is something which is still in prospect for earthly
humanity. Thus when he speaks of them, Rudolf Steiner has in
mind a distant future condition of humanity.[78] Although the first
symptoms of their gradual incursions into earthly evolution are
already making themselves felt here and there in modern civilization, nevertheless the principal task in our time remains above all
the knowledge of and the opposition to the ahrimanic powers, to
which Rudolf Steiner referred again and again right up to the end of
his earthly life.[79]

★

As we view the path of inner development summarized in this
chapter as a single whole, we may discern its remarkable connection
with the fundamental path of modern Christian-Rosicrucian
initiation as set forth by Rudolf Steiner in his book *Occult Science* and
in many lectures and lecture-cycles.[80] One could even say that what
has been described here is a kind of metamorphosis of this central
path of modern initiation.

We shall now, as the conclusion of this chapter, place this relationship before us in a single picture. The first stage of Christian Rosicrucian initiation—'the study of spiritual science with the help of an ordinary faculty of judgement such as has been won in the physical world'—will correspond to man's aspiration to attain through such studies a total transformation of his thinking, which includes acquiring the faculty of considering every phenomenon or being that one encounters in life from all twelve points of view. For only such a ceaseless projection of a many-sidedness into one's thinking—and an education of the senses that is based upon it— can serve as a foundation for a real *tolerance* with respect to all that comes from other people. The second stage of 'attainment of imaginative knowledge' will correspond to the practice or path of *forgiveness* which leads to an experience in Imagination of the Etheric Christ in the supersensible world nearest to the Earth (on the astral plane).

The third stage of 'inspirative knowledge' will correspond to taking on the karma of other people, one person or a small group, as takes place most notably in the case of the individual relationships between a spirit-teacher and his pupils. Rudolf Steiner refers to this stage of development in the following words of Benedictus from the third Mystery Play, *The Guardian of the Threshold*:

I must accompany each one
who has received from me on Earth
the spirit's light, whether he knew or not
that he became my pupil.
I have to lead him further on the way
which he through me began to walk in spirit.[81]

The fourth stage of 'intuitive knowledge' corresponds to taking upon oneself not only the karma of another individual or a small group of people but of a whole society, which in its various elements contains representatives of the whole of humanity, with the result that this represents the beginning of the initiate's participation in bearing the karma of mankind. The higher knowledge of Christ as the new Spirit of the Earth and, in addition, as the macrocosmic Ego who is directly present and works within his own ego, which is revealed to him at this stage, enables him, once he has attained this level of spiritual development, to begin the conscious work of liberating all three categories of opposing spirits through the power of the Christ Sun that has arisen within him. However, although the *possibility* of this is revealed to the initiate already at the fourth stage, nevertheless a real participation in this process becomes fully accessible to him only at subsequent, still higher, stages of spiritual development.

Thus by acquiring at the fifth stage of the Christian-Rosicrucian path a true 'knowledge of the relationship between microcosm and macrocosm' that has come about as a result of the union of the macrocosmic Being of Christ with the microcosmic being of the man Jesus of Nazareth—a union which reached its culmination at the Mystery of Golgotha—the initiate wins the power that can make it possible for Lucifer to turn to the good.

At the sixth stage, by achieving—while being still in the physical body—the capacity of 'becoming one with the macrocosm' and of living consciously within it, without thereby losing one's awareness of one's individuality even for a moment (and this is possible only where the human ego has been permeated by the Christ-impulse),[82] the initiate acquires the power that will, in time, turn also Ahriman towards the good.

Finally, in a still more distant future, having consciously attained that condition which Rudolf Steiner designates as the last, con-cluding, stage of the Christian-Rosicrucian path, the description of which (he says) lies beyond the limits of what a modern earthly language can express and ordinary human reason can understand,[83] the initiate will be in a position to exert some influence upon the third category of opposing beings. This will be possible for him only when the Christ-impulse that has been received by him into his ego also permeates his physical body, transforming it to an ever greater degree into the 'new Resurrection body', and at the same time leading his clairvoyant consciousness into the Kingdom of the Father, which extends right down to the material world. In other words, when the words of Christ 'No one comes to the Father but by me' (John 14:6) become for him a directly experienced occult reality.

Now that we have, in this chapter, characterized the position occupied by *forgiveness* in the context of that spiritual path of which it is so integral a part, we can take our study of it further.

VI

The Occult Significance of Forgiveness

1. The Fundamental Conditions of Forgiveness

As we endeavour to approach the problem of forgiveness from an occult point of view, it is necessary first of all to point out those signs by which true forgiveness may without fail be distinguished from the numerous guises and likenesses under which it often appears in life which do not bear any affinity to its real essence. In this sense, forgiveness is often understood too simply, for so often in life what may at a cursory glance appear to be forgiveness is really only a particular form of conscious or unconscious egoism—a hidden wish to present oneself in as advantageous a light as possible, to don a mask of false virtue. This so-called 'forgiveness' does not really make any great inner demands, even though it can easily be made use of for achieving some kind of self-seeking purpose.

In contrast to such pseudo-forgiveness, true forgiveness is characterized above all by two qualities or signs; these are especially evident in the second and fourth examples given in chapter III. We shall now consider these in reverse order. In the case of the fourth example, reference was made to the 'Appeal for Reconciliation' which Marie Steiner wrote in 1942. In this document, the first basic property of any true act of forgiveness is mentioned several times. Of this it is particularly important to be aware because it is precisely this which makes genuine forgiveness so difficult. Marie Steiner writes in this regard: 'The resolve to *overcome oneself* should be consciously taken hold of by the community. Clearly and willingly';[84] and then again at the end of the 'Appeal': 'Let us rescue his

[Rudolf Steiner's] work and human culture by overcoming ourselves and achieving reconciliation . . .'

In order that we may better understand the need for self-overcoming in every act of true forgiveness, we must take into consideration what we have already said regarding how in an act of forgiveness there takes place a permeation of the lower ego by the forces and substances of the higher ego. This is always associated with the need for man to be simultaneously overcoming all the tendencies of his lower ego which draw him down. For only where the forces of the latter have been overcome to a sufficient degree by the moral will of man can the higher ego unfold its activity. This means that true forgiveness always has a *sacrificial character*.

The extent of its occult effectiveness—of which more will be said later on—is determined in the first instance precisely by the extent of its *sacrificiality*, as expressed in the overcoming—albeit only partial—of the lower ego by the higher. For the lower ego, through the force of the egoism that constantly dwells within it, resists forgiveness in every possible way and clutches at any opportunity or excuse to avoid taking this inner step. By its very nature, man's lower ego is always inclined towards rancour and never has any wish to forget 'willingly'; it sees any deed of forgetting as something that inflicts harm upon its purely egoistic integrity (see chapter IV).

The second principal quality of true forgiveness is its inner activity. True forgiveness—as distinct from its false counterpart— can never have a passive character. For we do not simply take a decision to 'forget' the wrong or injustice that has been perpetrated upon us but, in addition, we take upon ourselves an inner obligation to *make amends* for that objective harm which the evil action has wrought not only upon us but also upon the world. In other words, in true forgiveness we willingly, out of complete inner freedom, take upon ourselves an inner obligation—to the extent that our forces permit—to give the world as much compassion, love and goodness as the evil action has objectively taken away from it.[85]

This second condition of true forgiveness appears with particular force in the second example, in the story of Bill Cody. 'Hate had just killed the six people who mattered most to me in the world,' he tells George Ritchie. 'I decided that I would spend the rest of my life—whether it was a few days or many years—loving every person I came in contact with.' Here we encounter a quite remarkable fact, namely, that this second condition is at one and the same time significantly more difficult and yet immeasurably easier than the first; it is more difficult from the standpoint of the lower ego but immeasurably easier from the standpoint of the higher ego. For in order to fulfil the first condition—a real overcoming of self—one has to work hard to gain a victory in the struggle between the higher ego and the lower, whereas in the case of the second condition it can be attained—if, of course, it can be fulfilled at all by a given person in a given life-situation—only *after* the achievement of this victory, that is, out of the *higher ego*.

If we now take into account that it belongs to the nature of the higher ego continually to forgive the lower ego—indeed throughout man's earthly life—and also to pour itself sacrificially into the surrounding world when, in permeating the lower ego, it is enabled to come in contact with the world, we can begin to understand those astonishing words spoken by Bill Cody, words which seem almost wholly improbable to our ordinary consciousness: 'It was an *easy decision*, really.' Indeed, what seems unfeasible and simply incomprehensible for the lower ego is for the higher ego something which stands to reason, something which is perfectly easy. Thus these words of Bill Cody about the 'ease of forgiveness' are the surest testimony that the higher ego was living and working in his soul.

What also follows from this example is that the 'difficulty' or 'ease' that a person has in achieving true, inwardly active, forgiveness is determined above all by the extent of the actual presence and activity within him of his higher ego, which means the degree of his mastery of his lower ego. In this sense, every person has in life an absolutely exact way—namely, through his capacity for forgiveness—of checking the extent of the presence and maturity within him of the higher ego.

In a remarkably exact way, this natural yearning of the higher ego to pour itself sacrificially into the world with which it comes in contact in the act of forgiveness has found its reflection in the corresponding word in the German language. This is the word *vergeben* ('forgive' in the sense of 'give away'), in which is contained both the inner gesture of *geben*, *schenken* ('giving, bestowing') and also *sich hingeben* ('self-surrendering')—that is, a total giving of oneself to the world in sacrificial love. As regards the first condition of forgiveness described above, it, too, has found its reflection in another German word, also having the meaning of 'forgiveness' but emphasizing a different aspect of it. This is the word *verzeihen* ('forgive' in the sense of 'excuse'), which comes from the word *verzichten* ('renounce'), expressing a voluntary repudiation of the egoistic forces and yearnings of the lower ego, which is possible only as a result of a real process of self-overcoming.

Thus in these two German words, which both mean forgiveness, we find that the genius of language has given us an impression of both these principle characteristics of true forgiveness: *verzeihen*, the overcoming of the lower ego by the higher (self-overcoming), and *vergeben*, the total outpouring (self-giving) of the higher ego to the world!

In this context the German language adopts a central position between West and East. Thus in English, French and Italian we have a word which in terms of its content and morphology cor-responds exactly to the German *vergeben*: English 'to forgive', French *pardonner*, Italian *perdonare*. The Russian verb *proshchats*, on the other hand, means 'to make simple, uncomplicated, natural', which entails a voluntary renunciation of everything that is com-plicated. In other words, the person who forgives returns to his original harmony with God, who in the mystical tradition of the Middle Ages is—in contrast to the world consisting of countless individual parts—a simple 'non-composite' being who therefore, from an esoteric point of view, has no karma. The growing distance of the whole of creation from the Creator is an effect of increasingly complex karmic laws and makes the world ever more complicated. Simplicity or uncomplicatedness as an expression of the fact that a person is to a high degree free from individual karma arising from human errors and imperfections was the original condition of Parsifal, who on that account was also called a 'holy fool'. To a certain extent *every* human individual experiences the feeling of relief and liberation which is always associated with the 'simplifying' of karma that goes with every act of true forgiveness; whereas bearing grudges weighs the soul down like a heavy burden.

★

Considering them more closely, it is possible to discern that both these fundamental conditions are to a certain extent in a diametrically polar relationship to one another. The first consists in the need to *forget* the wrong to which a person has been subjected, which is wholly impossible without a real self-overcoming. The second—as in the case of Bill Cody—consists (in contrast) in the ceaseless *remembering* of that inner promise, which is also inseparable from any true act of forgiveness and consists in voluntarily taking upon oneself an obligation to restore to the world as much goodness and love as were objectively removed from it by the evil or immoral action.

Two fundamental conditions of forgiveness—to forget a wrong to which one has been subjected and constantly to remember the need to bring love and goodness into the world as the sole means of overcoming the consequences of evil in the world—correspond *in life* to that stage of modern initiation which the spirit-pupil attains on his path of inner development when he reaches the 'temple of higher knowledge', and then receives the 'draught of forgetfulness' and the 'draught of remembrance'. 'This means that he is initiated into the secret of how to act without allowing himself to be continually disturbed by the lower memory ... He must be able to wipe out the veil of memory which envelops one at every moment of one's life.'[86] And through the second 'draught', '... he acquires the power to have higher mysteries constantly present in his consciousness ... They must become practice, habit, inclination.' These words do, indeed, characterize the actual experiences of the modern initiate at this stage. In the process of forgiveness they appear in a kind of metamorphosis which is the beginning of what Rudolf Steiner designates as 'a certain level of initiation which has already been unconsciously achieved in [ordinary] life.'[87] The effect of the first draught is manifested within man in the form of a consciously evoked forgetting (obliteration) of all negative inclinations of his lower ego, especially of all forms of rancour and envy; the effect of the second, in the form of an equally consciously evoked, ceaseless remembering of the presence in his soul of the forces of the higher ego, of its yearning to pour itself forth into the world in sacrificial love.

Finally, one further element which belongs without doubt to any true act of forgiveness is that of *knowledge* [or insight]. This appears with particular clarity in the story of Bill Cody. In his story he tells George Ritchie: 'I was a lawyer. In my practice I had seen too often what hate could do to people's minds and bodies.'

In order that we may understand these words, and also the fundamental role of knowledge in the process of forgiveness, it is necessary to turn again to its central archetype, the highest expression of *cognitive love* on the Earth, to the words of Christ on the Cross: 'Father, forgive them, for they know not what they do.' 'They know not ...' because, being wholly in the realm of activity of the lower ego alone, they are completely bereft of a knowledge of *who* stands before them. They do not even suspect that the man who is being crucified by them is indeed the Bearer of the World Ego, the Bearer of the higher, cosmic archetype of their own ego. What might otherwise have become for them the meaning and content of their whole lives they do not comprehend, for in their inner dullness they are at this moment utterly removed from any influences of their own higher ego, with whose eyes alone they might have been able to glimpse *who* was actually standing before them.

Thus in this historic scene on the Hill of Golgotha—where there are people who, in complete unawareness of who is standing before them, are crucifying Christ Jesus, who forgives them from the Cross (for He knows that if they had only recognized who was standing before them as the archetype of their own ego they would never have crucified Him but would rather have bowed down before Him and become His disciples)—we have at one and the same time a mystical and a historical archetype of the relationship of the lower and the higher ego in every human being who has not as yet attained to knowledge of the latter. For being without this knowledge and having an allegiance only to the lower ego and its egoistic motives, such a person is—in blindly following it—guilty before his own higher ego rather than before some fellow human being. Moreover, one could even say that, in giving himself up solely to the forces of his lower ego, he is, in essence, continually crucifying his higher ego in a spiritual sense, even though it nevertheless 'forgives' him, inasmuch as the person himself in his ordinary consciousness knows nothing about this state of affairs.

On the other hand, when a person forgives, in a more occult sense the opposite takes place. His higher ego, as it works in the act of forgiveness and permeates the lower ego with its substance, begins to lead it towards spiritual awakening, that is, to a *recalling* of those purposes and tasks which he put before himself in his higher ego *before* his birth on Earth, but which he completely forgot about once he had incarnated in a physical body.*

Plato (in the *Menon*) once called all true knowledge recollection (anamnesis). And if we consider the process of forgiveness from an occult point of view, this ancient truth can acquire for us an entirely new significance.

It is, of course, the case that in pre-earthly existence a human being sets himself the most diverse goals and tasks with respect to his impending incarnation. Which of these does he recall in the first instance in the process of forgiveness? He initially recalls those which then come to manifestation in the act of forgiveness itself. Thus he recalls the need in earthly life for a continual self-overcoming (an overcoming of his lower ego) and also for a sacrificial outpouring of self into the world in love. However, in the supersensible existence in which man dwells before his birth on Earth, in contrast to his earthly state of being, both these goals which have been set before him out of the higher ego exist not in the form of abstract ideals, or moral precepts or imperatives, but in the form of actual *beings* of the spiritual world, who embody the respective impulses in their whole essence.

Thus the motives for these two fundamental conditions of true forgiveness are apprehended by human beings in the spiritual world not abstractly but out of a direct contemplation of the beings

---

* The reason why he forgets about them after he has been born will be spoken of further in part 4 of this chapter.

(referred to above) whom every human individual of our time encounters in the higher world *before* his incarnation on Earth: Christ and His 'angelic countenance', Michael.[88]

Before his birth in the earthly world, man first encounters Michael, that high hierarchic spirit who is always and everywhere defying the dragon. As a result of this meeting there is revealed to him that power which he will need if on Earth he is to gain, in his own soul, the victory of the higher ego over the lower, provided that it is his wish to remain true to this archetype; this is the power of *self-overcoming*, which leads to the constant victory of the higher over the lower, and to its representative in our cosmos: Michael. As the 'spiritual champion of freedom',[89] he represents in the spiritual world that power which may perhaps best be expressed in words of human language in the following lines by Goethe from his unfinished poem, 'Secrets':

> In this inner storm and outer struggle
> The spirit hears what scarce it comprehends:
> The man who overcomes himself finds freedom
> From the power that binds all living creatures.

In these words we find an allusion to the path of the journey that we take—while still in earthly existence—towards the call of Michael, which in our epoch is directed towards every human being before his birth.

After Michael, it is Christ who appears to man in his pre-earthly existence. And as a result of beholding Him, a second, still higher, power is revealed to man, one which his soul will need on Earth if he has the wish to follow this still higher cosmic archetype. This is that power whose bearer in our cosmos is the Christ: the power of world sacrificial love. Thus Rudolf Steiner, drawing from the central stream of Christian esotericism, also calls Him the 'great sacrifice', the 'sacrificial Mystic Lamb'.[90]

★

As we have seen, true forgiveness is possible in the earthly world only on the foundation of these two powers in their microcosmic activity within man. Thus when we really forgive we are at the same time approaching the cosmic origins of these powers of whom our higher ego preserves for us a memory, for our higher ego was before our birth the servant of Michael-Christ[91] and wishes through forgiveness to continue the path of this service on the Earth.

2. Forgiveness and the Karmic Activity of Christ

Through an act of forgiveness we can also become on Earth the servants and mediators of Michael-Christ in another, quite different, direction. In order that we may better understand this, let us imagine what takes place from an occult point of view in the opposite case, in the event of non-forgiveness.

If an injury is inflicted or a wrong perpetrated on a certain person by another human being, the all-embracing laws of karma enter into operation at once. Their task is to call forth, sometimes in this life but more often in a subsequent life, a situation whereby both human beings meet again, though this time in such a way that the latter person, who stands guilty before the first, will now have to make amends for his action in some way or other, that is, to bring the first person just as much good in the new situation as he brought him evil in the former life.

If one takes into account the many-faceted and extraordinarily complex interweaving of individual human destinies on Earth, both as they concern the 'guilt' of one person towards another, an aspect which demands—as of necessity—karmic compensation, and also all the infinite karmic connections which unite the individual human being with his people and with mankind as a whole (with his epoch), it is not difficult to imagine what a truly colossal task— one that embraces our entire cosmos—the forces of karma have to undertake in order that *every* human deed, feeling or thought may sooner or later, with iron necessity, receive its due recompense.

Thus for the fulfilment of this all-embracing law of the iron necessity of karma, which is at the same time also the law of the higher justice of our cosmos, *all nine* divine-spiritual Hierarchies in the spiritual worlds must participate. Rudolf Steiner speaks about this as follows: 'This human karma is, at first, like a veil, a curtain. If we look behind this veil we gaze at the weaving deeds and influences of Archai, Archangeloi, Angeloi; Kyriotetes, Dynamis, Exusiai; Seraphim, Cherubim and Thrones.'[92] For all these Hierarchies, however, it is by no means a matter of indifference whether an individual forgives the person who stands guilty before him or has perpetrated some evil against him. If he does *not* forgive, he thereby—so to speak—'forces' the Hierarchies in future to form world karma, and the whole future evolution of the world and humanity that depends on it, in complete correspondence with the law of iron necessity, which calls forth sooner or later the just and sufficient compensation for every evil deed. The infinite spiritual powers of all nine Hierarchies must in this event be expended upon the fashioning of situations which enable this compensation to achieve fulfilment in earthly evolution. Hence it is possible to say that every refusal to forgive brings about the further strengthening of the net of the iron necessity of karma which envelops our cosmos.

On the other hand, if an individual forgives in the way that has been characterized in this book, he is thereby voluntarily renouncing that recompense to which he has an objective right in the cosmos for having suffered an unrequited wrong through another person's doing. And by renouncing the recompense that would surely have been bound to come his way in one of his subsequent earthly lives, such an individual liberates, by this step, truly boundless forces of the higher Hierarchies from the *necessity* of creating in the future, on the Earth, more new situations for the compensating of past karma.

Thus in the event of forgiveness, these forces of the higher Hierarchies are made *free*, which is to say that they can be used not in the sense of the laws of iron karmic necessity, but as higher spiritual forces which—through being freely sacrificed to the world—work on within it in a completely new form, one which from the standpoint of earthly evolution can be called 'grace'. In other words, the essential part of the spiritual forces which were formerly used by the Hierarchies for the fulfilment of the all-embracing law of karma is liberated from this task and may now be used in another way, namely, in the spirit of the intentions and purposes of Christ, as the building-stones for the new moral cosmos which He is gradually constructing and of which Rudolf Steiner speaks at the very end of his book *Occult Science*.[93] Because of this there gradually begins to arise, in the very heart of that realm of iron karmic necessity which permeates our entire cosmos, a new kingdom, a kingdom where karma becomes grace, where necessity is transformed into total spiritual freedom and where Christ Himself works as the *Lord of Karma*. For as a result of every act of true forgiveness, man as it were fashions in the web of karma a space which is not filled with karmic substance and into which Christ can then enter and work within it and, moreover, to which the luciferic and ahrimanic powers have no access.

Thus with every act of forgiveness, man transforms a part of the world field of karma, which envelops our cosmos with a dense net of iron necessity, into a new field of activity of Christ, as the Lord of Karma. As it is in our time that Christ becomes the Lord of Karma,[94] it follows that forgiveness will both in our time, and to an ever greater extent in the future, have an immeasurable significance for human evolution.

As regards the person who has forgiven, there arises for him in the act of forgiveness a completely new relationship of gradually becoming an ever more conscious colleague of Christ in the sphere of karma, that is, in the process of transforming our entire cosmos. And at the same time Christ Himself enters into the sphere of the actual forming of such a person's individual karma far more intensely than *without* this. Thus one can say that at the moment of forgiveness the principle 'Not I, but Christ in me' begins to become manifest in man, while in the event of non-forgiveness the opposite principal, 'Not I, but Jahve in me', appears in its stead. It follows from this that it is precisely in accordance with his capacity for forgiveness that every individual can establish as a living reality (and not merely in the realm of abstract thought) either to what extent he is a man of the Old Testament, one who lives solely by the laws of karmic necessity, forgiving nothing and no one ('Vengeance is mine, I will repay', Deuteronomy 32:35), or to what extent he has already embarked upon the path towards becoming a human being of the New Testament, opening out like a flower towards the Sun of the freedom, love and grace of Christ.[95]

This is directly associated with the mighty change which is taking place today in the spiritual world 'bordering upon the Earth', whereby the Etheric Christ is becoming the Lord of the karma of earthly evolution. Rudolf Steiner characterizes this change in the following way.

In olden times, each individual belonging to western civilization encountered after death, and before entering kamaloka, two supersensible figures: a cherub with a flaming sword similar to the one who had driven Adam and Eve out of Paradise, the representative of that cosmic justice which must be adhered to; and Moses with the Law Tables, which bring the powers of iron karmic necessity to visible manifestation.

According to the testimony of modern spiritual science, from our time onwards a third figure—the Christ—gradually joins these two figures and eventually takes the place of Moses. The appearance of Christ in Moses' stead does, however, mean that 'our karma enters into a relationship with Christ, Christ grows together with our own karma'.[96] This is—not in an abstract but a spiritually concrete sense—the transition from Old Testament to New Testament humanity referred to above. The free and conscious development of the capacity to forgive, which can significantly accelerate this transition, is an essential element of this process. This connection becomes clearly discernible through one fact in particular.

One of the most important consequences for the individual human soul of the transformation of the figure of Moses into that of Christ in the supersensible worlds will be that it will experience during earthly life what Rudolf Steiner describes as *the new karmic clairvoyance*. This represents a metamorphosis and further development of what is habitually called conscience. For what is in the case of most human beings audible as a more or less dim voice of conscience is gradually transformed into life-filled imaginative pictures, which reveal to the individual what he must accomplish in the future from a higher standpoint, that is, from the standpoint of his higher ego, in order to offset the consequences of wrongful deeds, feelings or thoughts.

As a result of such a supersensible vision, the individual—if he is able to understand it aright (and that will be possible as spiritual science becomes more widespread)—will say to himself: 'Now I have done this [some sort of wrongful deed]. I shall be shown what I must do to compensate for it, and what would hold me back in my unfolding perfection if I were not to make this compensation.'[97]

Such an experience is directly associated with what was cited in the previous chapter as the second condition of true forgiveness: bringing as much good into the world as was taken from it through the wrongful deed, the endeavour to compensate for the latter. This is, however, none other than the consequential widening and deepening of the impulse of conscience in the direction of the new karmic clairvoyance of which spiritual science speaks. As for the first condition, which is that the lower ego overcomes itself and con- sciously sacrifices all wishes and inclinations to the higher ego, the individual will necessarily have to fulfil this in order to develop the inner powers that he needs if he is to fulfil on Earth what was shown to him in imaginative vision. Thus these two preconditions of forgiveness are directly related to the modern mystery of the human conscience, with its gradual transformation into the new karmic vision and with the capacity of living in accordance with it.

Thus when he forgives, an individual gradually reaches out beyond his personal karma and increasingly frees himself from its compulsion. And at the same time he becomes on Earth that organ through which—as in the case of Bill Cody—Christ Himself, as the Lord of Karma, can work directly among mankind in etheric form. For the karma of one who has forgiven, which has not been lived out and is still seeking its final realization, is in the process of for- giveness being filled with new moral substance and acquires, as it were, a new content. Finally, a person is not thereby freed from the karmic consequences of the errors or evil deeds for which he has at one time or another been responsible but, through the active manifestation within him of the Christ-impulse, as a 'destiny- ordering power', all the trials, sufferings and shocks of destiny which necessarily fall to the lot of such a person become part of the general karma of the world and humanity in the sense of the intentions and purposes of Christ, and are at the same time directed by Him in such a way that for the person himself they serve merely to further the awakening and growth within him of the forces of the higher ego.

3. The Cosmic Archetype of Forgiveness

Rudolf Steiner often refers in his lectures to the problem of forgiveness in connection with the three-year life of Christ Jesus on the Earth, and particularly in the studies of the four Gospels which he gave to anthroposophists. In these latter lectures, Rudolf Steiner comments upon a whole series of New Testament scenes that are associated with this theme. For example, the story of the 'woman taken in adultery' (John 8:1–11), the scene of the healing of the paralytic (Matthew 9:2–8) and, finally, the conversation of Christ Jesus with the robber who was crucified at His right hand (Luke 23:39–43).[98]

In all these Gospel scenes where Christ Jesus, as the cosmic archetype of the ego-principle, brings about the 'forgiveness of sinners', what takes place from a spiritual-scientific point of view is that as a result of their meeting with Christ the ordinary ego of these people is for a shorter or longer period permeated by their higher ego. Thus in the first of the scenes referred to, the power of Christ contained in the words 'Let him who is without sin among you be the first to throw a stone at her' calls forth, in all those who have brought the woman there, the awakening of their higher ego, that is, a dim awareness of the profound guilt before it of their own lower ego. After this, the Gospel tells us, 'being accused by their conscience they went away one by one' (John 8:9). The voice of conscience here is none other than the voice within their souls of the higher ego, whose forces—once they have been awakened by Christ—begin henceforth to prevail over their lower ego (which still lives in the sphere of the law: 'Now Moses in the law commanded us to stone such people', John 8:5) by permeating and transforming it. As a result of this, there is 'no one' among those who had come 'who condemns' (John 8:10) the woman; all, in clear contradiction of the law, forgive her.

In a similar way, Christ also awakens the forces of the higher ego

within the paralytic. In the words which He employs as He turns to
him, 'Take heart, my son!' (Matthew 9:2), the very word 'son' refers
to the beginning of the working within the sick man of his higher
ego. For, as the Son of God, Christ represents the Ego of the
macrocosm, and, as the Son of Man, the higher ego of every human
being. Then it is not Christ Himself but the higher ego of the
paralytic, permeated by the power that proceeds from Him, which
accomplishes in him once again what it achieves within every
human being in earliest childhood before the awakening of individual ego-consciousness; it brings about that 'rising and walking'
(Matthew 9:5) whereby a child is endowed with the capacity to
stand and walk in an upright position for the rest of its life.

The whole contrast between the conduct of a man who is acting
out of the impulses of the higher ego and one who is acting out of
the impulses of the lower ego appears with particular clarity in the
scene of the Crucifixion itself, in the relationship of the two
criminals to Christ Jesus: the one turning to Him and the other
speaking ill of Him. In this scene we have a grand prophetic imagination of the future division of humanity into two races, the good
and the evil, which is being prepared already in our time but which
will be manifested to its full extent only in the sixth cultural epoch
and will reach its culmination on Jupiter.[99] At the foundation of
such a division will lie the direct relationship of *every* individual
human being to Christ. Already in our time, though especially—as
has been observed—from the sixth epoch onwards, an ever larger
number of people will be honoured with a direct supersensible
vision of Christ in the etheric body and in full freedom will then be
placed before the choice of receiving or rejecting Christ. It is this
wholly free decision which determines the further path of such a
soul, whether it belongs to the good or the evil race.

Rudolf Steiner considers this case of 'forgiveness of sins' at some
length in the penultimate lecture of the cycle *Christ and the Human
Soul*, where, with this scene as a background, he reveals to his listeners one of the most central facts of anthroposophical Christology.
What he says is as follows: both the criminals who are being crucified on the right and the left hand of Christ have committed
identical crimes, and both of them, according to the inexorable law

of karma, will in future earthly lives have to erase all their consequences to the full. How, then, can it be that in this case Christ forgives one of them? In order to answer this question, Rudolf Steiner points to the dual nature of the karmic consequences which arise as a result of the deeds wrought by man. Firstly, there are those actions which relate to man himself and which will gradually be fully atoned for by man through the working of the laws of karma; and secondly, there is objective evil, which with every wrongful deed brings harm to the world. A simple example may serve to explain this. If one human being has in life tormented and inflicted pain upon another, then according to the law of karma he will in one of his subsequent incarnations have to bring to the person he has afflicted as much good as he brought to him by way of harm in this life. Nevertheless, as an objective event, the very fact that he has subjected another person to torments has already become part of the world process. As this has for all eternity been inscribed in the Akashic Record, into the ineradicable spiritual memory of our cosmos, it continues to work on in the world as—albeit in a small way—a centre of destructive forces. And if nothing besides this were to happen, then by the end of the present phase of earthly evolution the following would have taken place. Even if all human individuals had been fully able to erase their personal *subjective* karma, the Earth itself, weighed down by the burden of the destructive forces preserved within the Akashic Record, as the *objective* consequences of the evil deeds, feelings and thoughts of people, would not be able to make the transition to Jupiter: 'Then human beings would arrive at the end of the Earth period with their karma balanced out, but the Earth would not be ready to develop into the Jupiter condition; the whole of Earth humanity would be there without a dwelling-place, without the possibility of developing on towards Jupiter.'[100] Moreover, the person concerned would then have to continually behold all his bad deeds, with their destructive consequences for the Earth and the entire cosmos, in the Akashic Record and experience from viewing them thus, and especially from the complete impossibility of atoning for them, the greatest of torments. This means that, while through karma man can redeem himself, he is unable out of his own forces alone to redeem the Earth—which is absolutely necessary for all subsequent evolution.

However, it is precisely here that Christ comes to man's help. For, having united Himself as a result of his passing through the Mystery of Golgotha with the Earth and with the whole of its human population, Christ, the new Spirit of the Earth, is, through His cosmic sacrifice, in a position quite literally to take upon Himself all the *objective* consequences for the world of our sins and errors and, hence, to blot out all their traces, even the very memory of them, from the Akashic Record. 'For through the fact of Christ's death on Golgotha, human beings will not see the tablets of their guilt and sin, but they will see Him who has taken them upon Himself; they will see, united in the Being of Christ, all that would otherwise be spread out in the Akashic Record. In place of the Akashic Record, the Christ stands before them, having taken all upon Himself.'[101]

And so, through the power of His sacrifice, Christ creates in the Akashic Record, in place of the evil deeds of human beings and their consequences that are inscribed therein, what could be described as 'empty spaces' which He then fills with His Earth-redeeming *Spirit*. Thus in the scene where this gift of the objective redemption of the Earth is given over to the Apostles before they are sent forth into the world, Christ Himself 'breathes' into them the Holy Spirit, renewing thereby the mystery of the primordial creation of man as described at the beginning of the Old Testament (Genesis 2:7). In St John's Gospel, this event is related as follows: 'And when He had said this, He breathed on them, and said to them, "Receive the Holy Spirit. If you forgive the sins of any, they are forgiven; if you retain the sins of any, they are retained"' (20:22–23). Rudolf Steiner makes the following further observations about this new working of the Holy Spirit: 'What does it signify for the human soul when one who may so speak says in the name of Christ: "Your sins are forgiven"? It means that he is able to assert: You have indeed to await the karmic consequences of your deeds, but Christ has transformed your guilt and sin in such a way that later on [i.e. on Jupiter] you will not have to bear the terrible sorrow of looking back upon your guilt and seeing that through it you have destroyed a part of the Earth's existence.'[102] And then Rudolf Steiner tells us that these words from the Gospel about the forgiveness of sins by the power of Christ are not of 'karmic' but of 'cosmic' significance.

However, man must—from our time onwards—consciously participate in this gradual transition from 'karmic' to 'cosmic' bonds or laws, or (which is in this case the same thing) from Earth to Jupiter. He must learn to care not only about his own redemption, to take an interest not only in his personal (subjective) karma, but also to concern himself with the redemption of the entire Earth, which is inseparably connected with the balancing out of its *objective* karma by means of the power of the Christ-impulse which he has received. For this, a person needs to transcend the bounds of his own individual karma, and that means above all learning to *forgive*.

At the same time, he must strive with all his forces towards what will become fully manifest only on Jupiter, when the 'feeling of community with the world ... will be of fundamental importance'[103] and when in the life which human beings have in common what Rudolf Steiner describes as the higher 'community of the Spirit' will become a reality—where the happiness and well-being of an individual human being will be impossible without the happiness and well-being of all.[104]

With this, we are now ready to answer the principal question of this chapter: Where do we find the *cosmic archetype* of the inner process which takes place in that moral act which on Earth is called *forgiveness*?

We have already spoken (see chapter IV) of how in the process of forgiveness man consciously erases, with a moral effort of his will, those memories which have to do with the wrongs that have been inflicted upon him from the unbroken stream of memory that flows continually through his ordinary ego and sustains all that he does in normal waking life. If, however, he is to accomplish this without inflicting harm upon his ordinary ego, he must work out of his higher ego or Spirit Self. In *Theosophy* Rudolf Steiner calls this latter member 'the *spirit* living as an ego',[105] the substance of which then fills the inner spaces of memory that are thus freed from the negative impressions from the past and, carrying with it moral intuitions, provides the possibility of turning all evil into good.

But Christ continually accomplishes this very same thing, though in the macrocosm, as He works in the aura of the Earth since the Mystery of Golgotha. He too, as the Representative of the higher Ego of our cosmos, ever and again erases from the stream of cosmic memory—from the Akashic Record—the consequences of all the objective evil inflicted by human beings upon the world, which is to say primarily upon Christ Himself, who—as the new Spirit of the Earth—has since the Mystery of Golgotha taken upon Himself the karma of the whole of mankind. The 'space' which has thus been made free in the Akashic Record Christ then fills with His Spirit, the new Holy Spirit that proceeds from Him,[106] which transmutes all 'karmic' facts into 'cosmic' facts, and the Earth into Jupiter.

Thus we can say: When we forgive, we accomplish on a small scale what Christ is continually accomplishing on a large scale. For just as Christ is continually erasing in the Akashic Record the consequences of our evil deeds, feelings and thoughts *for the world*, so in forgiving do we ourselves become like Him in this, as we erase through our higher ego the wrongs that have been inflicted upon us from the memory-stream of our ordinary ego.

While Christ, as He fills with His Spirit the spaces that He has freed within the Akashic Record, is thereby preparing the future moral space of Jupiter, man is, as he imitates Him, even now learning with every act of true forgiveness to *live in the conditions of the future Jupiter*, in the conditions of its moral space.

Thus every individual who understands the meaning and purpose of the evolution of the world and of humanity in the spirit of the intentions of the living Christ is called to concern himself not only with the aims of his own limited existence but also to 'further the divine purpose appointed for the Earth',[107] by developing within himself those forces of forgiveness which make him a participant in the cosmic process of the forming by Christ—in the very heart of Earth evolution—of the embryo of the future Jupiter.

4. *The Influence of Forgiveness upon Man's Life after Death*

In any human conflict, where, on the one hand, an evil or unjust deed is wrought and, on the other hand, its forgiveness, there immediately arises an inner polarization, which consists in the strengthening of the forces of the lower ego in one of the participants and of the forces of the higher ego in the other. And at the same time, in accordance with the fundamental pedagogical law referred to above, there emerges the possibility of a direct influence of the higher ego (Spirit Self) of the one person upon the lower ego of the other, extending even to the latter's karmic roots. Even if this cannot be manifested outwardly in earthly life through a personal meeting between the two human beings, the act of forgiveness will in any case, quite irrespective of whether the person who has been forgiven is aware of this in his ordinary consciousness, nevertheless have considerable significance for his life *after death*.

In order that we may gain a better understanding of the nature of the influence of forgiveness upon man's life after death, it is necessary to recall that Rudolf Steiner speaks about the effects in our time of two kinds of etheric bodies of dead people in the spiritual world nearest to the Earth. To the first category belong the etheric bodies of people who in their last earthly life were under the prevailing influence of modern materialistic civilization, especially the etheric bodies of those who have given themselves up to nationalistic ideas and passions. For nothing so promotes the darkening and hardening of man's etheric body as any form of nationalism living in his soul. However, a similar effect is made upon man's etheric body by an active unwillingness to forgive, appearing as it does in any form of rancour or envy, which themselves also have a considerable hardening and darkening influence upon the etheric body. For, like the nationalist, a person filled with rancour lives in negative ideas which, despite being permeated with concentrated will-forces, are wholly fixed and have a powerful effect upon his etheric body; and these ideas eventually become centres in the etheric body around which a 'densification' of etheric substance is continually taking place. Subsequently, after the death of such people, their etheric bodies do not dissolve at once in the surrounding world ether but— like the etheric bodies of nationalists—can be made use of by ahrimanic spirits in their battle against the appearance of the Etheric Christ in the spiritual world nearest to the Earth.[108] In contrast, people who are particularly inclined towards forgiveness bring an influence to bear upon their etheric bodies such that they dissolve very rapidly in the general world ether after their death. Because of this, such people are in their after-death existence easily able to find the path to the hosts of Michael, which battle under his leadership in the spiritual world nearest to the Earth for the right—undistorted—appearance of Christ to humanity and for the consolidation of His authority among men against the ill-dissolving human etheric bodies referred to above and the ahrimanic demons that work through them.

In the whole series of lectures which he gave during the First World War, Rudolf Steiner refers in particular to people of Eastern European origin as being those whose etheric bodies dissolve especially quickly after their death in the etheric environment of the Earth, which leads to their becoming Michael's chief helpers in his battle for the appearance of the Etheric Christ.[109] This observation of Rudolf Steiner's finds its full confirmation in the wholly non-nationalistic character of the Eastern European people (Rudolf Steiner speaks in this connection about the 'exceptionally cosmopolitan' element of the Russians),[110] and also in their remarkable capacity for forgiveness, this being indeed one of the central features of their character—as has been repeatedly shown over the course of their history, including our present century.

If we now again recall that in the process of forgiveness a person's higher ego (Spirit Self), or—which is the same thing—his Guardian Angel, has a far more direct influence upon his ordinary ego, we begin to understand why it is that those individualities who have in their previous life passed through an incarnation in an Eastern European body are enabled after death 'to identify in consciousness with their Angel, to behold the spiritual world as though ... with the eyes of the Angel.'[111] And he continues: 'For those who belong to the Russian people it is perfectly natural to be in constant companionship with their Angel ... to grow together with the Angel ...'

However, a relationship of this kind with one's Angel after death is something which exists not only in 'Russian' souls but, in the light of all that has been said, can justly be related to the after-death existence of *every* human being (irrespective of what nation he belongs to) who develops in his soul a capacity for true forgiveness or—to put it more simply—has forgiven much in his previous earthly life.

★

There is in life one further highly important form of forgiveness, which is directed not towards another person or a group of human beings but towards the harsh destiny that has befallen someone and which comes to expression, for example, in a serious incurable illness or a misfortune whose consequences have to be borne until the end of life. Instances of this could include an innocent person spending many years in prison or in a concentration camp.

Such experiences as these can of course arouse an inner protest in one's soul, indignation, despair, inner resignation; or, on the other hand, they can lead one to a complete *reconciliation* with one's destiny, relating to it as to a trial that has been sent from above. This unreserved acceptance of one's destiny can even be transmuted in one's soul into a feeling of gratitude with regard to the higher powers of existence.

We have here to do with an altogether special form of forgiveness which—allowing, of course, for the inadequacy of our earthly language for such notions—could be called the 'forgiveness of one's own destiny'. In a case of such a total acceptance of one's destiny, just as in a case of true forgiveness, there takes place a highly intense permeation of the lower ego by the higher. For any incurable illness that has arisen as a result of one's karma, or a misfortune which leads to an abrupt change in the course of one's life, are the direct result of those higher decisions which one has *oneself* made in the spiritual world, when one was abiding in one's higher ego (Spirit Self) before finally descending to earthly incarnation. At that time one made these decisions, on the one hand, out of a contemplation of all the beauty and sublimity of the divine-spiritual cosmos and, on the other, through observing all the inadequacies and imperfections of one's own being as it has emerged from past lives, in order that these may be amended through voluntarily—from the standpoint of the higher ego—undergoing the corresponding spirit-purifying and spirit-enabling trials in a future earthly life. And so now on Earth, through voluntarily accepting and being reconciled with these trials and overcoming the fear, despair and protest of one's ordinary ego, one is again carried by the higher ego that brings about these trials. Henceforth only one's *own* impulse works within one, or—as it could also be called—the impulse of one's Guardian Angel, with whom a person who has overcome himself and accepted his destiny enters into the kind of direct relationship that was described above in the example of the after-death existence of the Russian (or East-European).

Herein lies one of the deeper historical reasons for the extra-ordinary amount of suffering, torment and tragic trials that have fallen to the lot of the peoples of Eastern Europe throughout their history and especially in the twentieth century. For 60 million sacrificial deaths in a single nation within the 72 years of the Bol-sheviks' rulership in Eastern Europe is a tragedy without parallel in the whole previous history of earthly humanity.

From this it becomes understandable why true forgiveness, as with the total acceptance of one's destiny, is so often connected with considerable difficulties. For in any act of true forgiveness one must necessarily pass through one particular agonizing experience which can last for a shorter or a longer time, though no one can avoid it, namely, an experience of inner *powerlessness*. This feeling has its source in that any act of true forgiveness is connected with a real repudiation of the 'desire for vengeance', which is to say, of any 'help' on the part of world karma. One could also say that in for-giveness there comes most powerfully to expression a total rejection of any form of 'claim to power' in the sphere of destiny (karma), so that one becomes in time completely defenceless before its blows and before the whole world that surrounds one.

From a spiritual-scientific point of view this circumstance arises through the fact that in the process of forgiveness there comes, as a rule, a moment when all the forces of the lower ego have with-drawn and there is as yet no experience of the higher ego—it has not as yet become fully manifested. A situation arises where one seeks to rise in the process of forgiveness from the earthly to the heavenly—from the lower ego to the higher—but is unable to do so. This condition is one of utter torment. But if one continues to make efforts and exert one's moral will, this sense of powerlessness is inwardly overcome and, like the rays of the Sun suddenly breaking through dense clouds, the victorious activity of the higher ego makes itself felt within one's soul.

What then takes place within one becomes a kind of micro-cosmic soul-spiritual experience of the Mystery of Golgotha, the result of which is that one begins to feel the direct presence of the living Christ within one's soul. Rudolf Steiner describes this passing through an inner condition of powerlessness and resurrection in the following words: 'But if we are able to experience powerlessness and a release from this sense of powerlessness, it transpires that we have the good fortune to have a truly real relationship to Christ Jesus ... And the person who is able to speak of these two events, of powerlessness and resurrection from powerlessness, is speaking of a real Christ experience.'[112] Thus the act of forgiveness can itself lead one to a real experience of Christ in one's own soul.

★

As we return to a consideration of that particular aspect of for-giveness which is manifested in the form of a total acceptance of one's destiny, it should be observed that such a relationship to it is possible not only for an individual but also for a whole people. For not only an individual but also an entire people or even a group of peoples can accept and be reconciled with a trial that has been sent from above, always ultimately having its origin in the karma of humanity as a whole, with the result that the tragic destiny of such a people becomes for it a real path of service to the higher Ego of all earthly humanity, Christ Himself. Every nation that accepts and bears its historical destiny without complaining, however onerous it may be, is following such a path of imitation of Christ.[113]

As regards the individual human being, the capacity for for-giveness and for complete acceptance of one's own destiny has for him one further highly important consequence—namely, that a person who has developed this capacity within himself has after his death an easy passage through the period of purification, a particularly light-filled kamaloka. For the significance of the latter consists in breaking the attachment to wrongful inclinations towards the purely physical world, in a kind of 'forgetting' of them; and a person who has forgiven much while on the Earth will thereby have developed a powerful inner capacity for 'soul oblivion', for a forgetfulness of what from the standpoint of the higher ego—in which man lives after death—should no longer remain in his soul.

For such a person, once his etheric body has separated off and—with it—his subjective memories of the earthly life that is now past have disappeared and the objective consequences of this life have been revealed in kamaloka (which down to the minutest detail have been preserved in the Akashic Record),[114] the following experience arises. As he beholds his past earthly life in the Akashic Record, he perceives in place of every act of forgiveness that he has accomplished on the Earth what could be described as the emergence of a free 'space' which, to the extent that he observes it closely, is gradually filled with the substance of Christ. To put this more simply, one could say that in the place of all the acts of forgiveness accomplished by him in the course of his past earthly life there appears to him Christ Himself. And this direct encounter with Christ can lead to such a person becoming after his death *already in kamaloka* His servant and envoy, the emissary of His will and mercy with respect to other human souls for whom their kamaloka is particularly difficult, and—above all—towards those whom he has forgiven with his whole heart on Earth, irrespective of whether or not those who have been forgiven by him had any knowledge of this in physical life.

For in every true act of forgiveness the process has already begun whereby one person (he who forgives) takes on the karma of another (he who has been forgiven). This enables the former, after the death of both, to become for the latter—during his period in kamaloka—a radiant guiding star on his murky spiritual horizon. Then at the behest of Christ Himself one soul appears before the other in order to guide it towards an awakening in the spiritual light of self-knowledge; for a soul that does not wish to acknowledge its guilt and to take upon itself all the consequences of its mistakes, errors, evil deeds, feelings and thoughts is doomed to experience the greatest sufferings in kamaloka. But it is precisely in real self-knowledge and in a true (from the standpoint of the higher ego and the spiritual cosmos) estimation of all that has been accomplished in physical life that another soul can help such a soul once it has for-given it on Earth. Now, in appearing before it at the behest of Christ, that is, bearing within itself the archetype of the higher ego of every human being, it can, as His ambassador, awaken in the other soul a clear consciousness of all its mistakes, errors and evil deeds, and springing from this consciousness, the growing faculty of perceiving in the spiritual light.

Moreover, through appearing in kamaloka to the soul of the person who has been forgiven, the soul of the forgiver can as a result of the act of forgiveness which it has accomplished on the Earth indicate to the other soul the path to the cosmic sphere of the Christ. For such is the spiritual power of true forgiveness: it gives the soul of the forgiver the power after death to bear within itself the light of Christ, that light which awakens the forces of the higher ego within all souls, not only those abiding in kamaloka but also those still living on the Earth.

Thus in forgiving, one receives the Christ-impulse into one's soul while still on Earth in such a way that—as took place in the case of Bill Cody—one can send forth a blessing upon all one's immediate surroundings, and after death can guide the forces of the Christ Sun into spiritual existence as a whole (enveloped as it is by a web of karmic laws), participating and helping in their gradual transfor-mation into blessing and love.

★

There is one further aspect of the effect of the forces of forgiveness after death which must be considered in this chapter. This is that the evil actions, mistakes and errors that have been perpetrated on the Earth call forth within man an ever greater preponderance of the lower ego over the higher, a kind of soul-spiritual eclipse. This means that the Guardian Angel who works within man through his higher ego gradually ceases to be able to guide the human beings entrusted to him any further. This happens with particular force immediately after the death of the person who has committed this wrongful act and who is at this time—at any rate for a certain period—almost wholly bereft of higher guidance.

In accordance with the laws pertaining in the spiritual world, the Guardian Angel has after a person's death the principal task of bringing his life after death into harmony or at least into a certain degree of correspondence with the spiritual cosmos as a whole—this being the chief condition for the *right* life of the human soul after death. However, if the human soul is in its after-death existence burdened with too great a weight of negative karma and, moreover (as often happens in such cases), is resisting self-knowledge—that is, the beholding of its own guilt—with all its forces, it is threatened by tormenting, unendurable inner sufferings called forth by its continued disharmony with the cosmos.

Subjectively, this new condition is experienced in such a way as though the spiritual world that now surrounds the soul were driving it back into the dark regions of kamaloka, which the Gospel calls those of 'outer darkness' (Matthew 8:12). As a result, its posthumous torments and—above all—the total 'cosmic solitude' that is brought about by being separated from its Angel continue to become more and more intense and can ultimately attain such a power that the soul is altogether deprived of any sense of time, that is, of all sense of a gradual ascent to the higher regions of the spiritual world, and its condition is subjectively experienced by it as 'eternal'. To a certain extent this can be compared with an experience of an infinite, and utterly empty, lifeless space where there is no movement, no development, a space that is wholly devoid of time. This is the source of the medieval idea of 'eternal' damnation or 'eternal' torment after death, which has unfortunately not as yet been revised or considered in the light of spiritual science by either the Eastern or the Western churches.

The sense of time in after-death existence, which is associated with an experience of a steady, harmonious growth into ever wider and more exalted circles (spheres) of the spiritual cosmos, is a quality that is bestowed upon the soul by its Angel, for that is the most essential aspect of his guardianship of the soul after death. However, someone who during earthly life has perpetrated a large number of evil deeds (or worse crimes) cannot be approached by his Angel, who is hence deprived of the possibility of fulfilling the task with which he is entrusted. Then, as he is not in a position to guide such a person on through the stages of the ascending spheres of the spiritual world, his Angel—to express it in more earthly language—so to speak *forgets* for a time the person entrusted to his guidance. In this case, being deprived of any kind of orientation in the spiritual worlds, such souls—in their efforts to do everything possible to escape from the unendurable suffering referred to above—often turn for help to demonic beings and, in exchange for a partial diminishing of their sufferings, rapidly find themselves fully in their power and then have to serve them in the spiritual sphere nearest to the Earth, introducing and spreading from thence in the physical world illnesses, epidemics, misfortunes and, in particular, furthering the diffusion of all manner of inclinations towards evil in the souls of earthly men.[115]

Thus in the very process of an Angel's temporary forgetting after death of the human being entrusted to him, there is a repetition *on a small scale* of what had once—in the Lemurian epoch—taken place with humanity as a whole on Earth as a result of the so-called 'Fall'. What in the case that has been referred to takes place with regard to the human soul after death occurred in the distant past of earthly evolution within the whole of humanity on the physical plane as a real fact. Thus, in describing—in the lecture of 14 August 1917—the consequences of this 'Fall' in the Lemurian epoch for mankind as a whole, Rudolf Steiner refers to how one must 'for human beings from ancient times until the Mystery of Golgotha pronounce these tragic words: "and the Gods forgot men".'[116] And if the Mystery of Golgotha had not happened, humanity would gradually have been blotted out from the memory of the divine-spiritual Hierarchies and would ultimately have succumbed forever to the influence of luciferic and ahrimanic spirits, as takes place in our time—although in an increasing majority of cases only temporarily—with particularly evil souls after their death. However, Rudolf Steiner goes on to say in the same lecture: 'one must say for the time since the Mystery of Golgotha: And the Gods *want* gradually to remember mankind once more.'

What has just been said can also be expressed as follows. As a result of the Gods' forgetting of human beings, the latter have in due course completely lost their connection with the spiritual stream of time and have been transformed on Earth into purely spatial beings—which would ultimately have led them to an ever greater inner degradation and also to physical extinction. But Christ, by descending to the Earth from the higher worlds, has (in Rudolf Steiner's words) 'restored time to human beings'.[117] According to modern spiritual research, Christ Himself spoke to 'His intimate disciples' about this in the following words: 'I . . . must tell you that I have come from the Sun . . . from the time which receives man only when he dies,' that is, from the 'stream of time' which flows 'from eternity to eternity'.[118]

It is precisely this introduction by Christ through the Mystery of Golgotha of the principle of time into earthly evolution which has aroused among the Gods the *will* once more to remember earthly humanity and, with it, the wish to become united with those human beings who have since that time—through receiving the Christ-impulse into themselves—sought a direct connection with the stream of spiritual time which permeates the entire world of the higher Hierarchies.

One further important consequence of the forgetting of mankind by the Gods was the loss by human beings on Earth of all memory of their existence in the spiritual worlds before their birth in the physical world. For there are two processes which are in the profoundest sense interrelated: the Gods forgot man, and man, as a result, forgot his life in the spiritual world before birth. However, this state of affairs also has its positive side. Through this 'forgetting' man acquired on Earth the inner foundation for the experience of freedom and also an inclination towards forgetting in his ordinary life. Thus since Lemurian times, and especially since the end of the Atlantean age, man's earthly memory has entered into an ever greater decline. This plays a truly enormous part in contributing towards the health of our physical organism, which continually derives forces of regeneration and renewal from those inner forces which are liberated within our etheric bodies through our continual forgetting about much that has happened to us in the past. Hence that 'forgetfulness' which often so annoys and impedes us in so far as our ordinary ego is concerned is actually beneficial for our physical body.[119] After all, if the Gods had not forgotten us, we would remember absolutely the whole of our past during earthly life, which is to say, we would have constantly before us that panorama of our past life which every individual otherwise beholds only in the first days after death, in the period which lasts until the eventual dissolution of his life body in the world ether. Such a condition, if experienced *already in earthly life*, would not only be destructive for the physical body (which in our time, as a result of modern materialistic civilization, has become hard and brittle and would therefore need a quite special inner preparation for such experiences, which would be achieved only in modern initiation) but would rule out the possibility of man's finding individual freedom on Earth—one of the most important achievements of earthly evolution.

Moreover, if the Gods had not forgotten mankind, if, that is, they had not loosened their connection with mankind as expressed through its consciousness, the memory of earthly man would have continued to be diffused not only through soul conditions like the panorama of life in the first days after death but also through further conditions like kamaloka. In other words, everything that man experiences unconsciously during sleep, as a kind of preparatory kamaloka,[120] would also have entered directly into his consciousness during the day.

The last traces of such a conscious experience of kamaloka were still preserved in the general evolution of humanity until the early period of the evolution of Greek culture. For the ancient Greeks this experience was manifested in clairvoyant visions of spiritual beings such as Erynies, Furies and Eumenides, who pursued anyone who had committed a crime not after death but during earthly life itself, as was the case, for example, with Orestes. Similar descriptions which have reached us from ancient Greek mythology are an indication to us of such remnants of the Gods' 'memory' of humanity, though often perceived only in a distorted form.[121] Examples of a similar kind can also be found in large measure in the Old Testament.[122]

Subsequently, this 'memory' of the Gods lived on among mankind only in the form of the ever weaker and more abstract 'voice of conscience', which was necessary in order that the thread connecting human beings with the Gods might not be completely broken.[123] However, from our time onwards, the process of the remembering of humanity by the Gods—which was begun by the Mystery of Golgotha—will, because of the entry of the Etheric Christ into earthly evolution, have to extend to the human conscience, gradually transforming it into a new faculty of karmic vision.[124] Only through this new visionary faculty will man be able to become, in time, a conscious collaborator with Christ in the sphere of karma (see chapter VI, 5).

★

Thus as a result of the fulfilment by Christ of the Mystery of Golgotha and His subsequent union with the Earth and with humanity, the Gods have again acquired an interest in man. In other words, in the course of their contemplation of the Mystery of Golgotha and its consequences the *will* has arisen within them to remember earthly human beings. However, while this will was enkindled within them through their contemplation of the sacrificial deed of Christ, the establishing of the conditions for its fulfilment, that is, for the emergence in the world of a new union and a conscious collaboration between the Gods and men, depends entirely upon the latter. And upon whether or not human beings have the wish to reach out towards this awakening will of the Gods for collaboration with them will depend the whole future evolution and further destiny of mankind. As the conscious coming together of Gods and men is possible only on the foundation of the gradual development by the latter of the forces of the higher ego, it follows that modern spiritual science or Anthroposophy has a truly central part to play in this process. It was for this reason that Rudolf Steiner characterized it in the following words: 'Anthroposophy is a knowledge which is brought forth from the higher self.'[125]

From this the significance of the role that true forgiveness is called upon to play in the gradual coming together of Gods and men becomes more comprehensible, inasmuch as it is, as we have seen, associated in a very direct way with the awakening and the working within man of his higher ego. One could say that, by forgiving, humanity creates both a real possibility and the most favourable conditions for the Gods to remember it. It is in this sense that we should understand those words from the Gospel of St Matthew which represent Christ's commentary on the Lord's Prayer which He had just given to His disciples: 'For if you forgive others their trespasses, your heavenly Father will also forgive yours; but if you do not forgive the trespasses of others, neither will your Father forgive your trespasses' (6:14–15). In other words, if you forgive others for their mistakes, the heavenly Father, that is in this case the whole company of the divine-spiritual Hierarchies,[126] will be able to remember you and thus receive you into His sphere, while if you do not forgive, the act of remembrance will not take place and you will then remain outside divine-spiritual existence.

If one bears in mind that the process of the forgetting of human beings by the Gods was brought about in the first place by the 'Fall' of man, it will be clear that in true forgiveness the human soul itself is now gradually beginning to overcome the consequences of this primal sin. For in forgiving, we once again restore both in our soul and in the world that surrounds us the higher Christ order which was lost by the soul as a result of the Fall. And what the soul of the person who has forgiven is able to accomplish after his death with regard to the person who has been forgiven on Earth and is now in kamaloka then becomes a continuation of this, albeit in a different form. Such a soul can then, at Christ's behest, appear as His messenger, and at the same time as the representative of the higher ego to the soul suffering in kamaloka and bring to it tidings of the connection which it has lost with the divine Kingdom of time, with the Kingdom of the ascending divine-spiritual Hierarchies—as a result of which its Angel is again able to approach (one could also say 'remember') it. This means that the soul that has itself attained through forgiveness a particularly deep connection with the Kingdom of the Angels is now able to help another soul, which has temporarily lost this connection, to find it again.

Thus in the life after death the forces of forgiveness can serve as a bridge between the human soul which, because of its evil deeds, has been deprived of higher guidance in the spiritual worlds and its Angel, thus restoring to him the possibility of guiding the soul entrusted to him from one incarnation to another, on a path of ascending evolution. By this means, forgiveness acquires a significance not merely for human existence but also for the life of Angels.

5. Forgiveness as a Socially Formative Power

The most important influence that an act of forgiveness can have on the earthly life of mankind is its influence upon the social sphere. This has already been briefly mentioned in chapter II, in considering the fourth petition of the 'Lord's Prayer', which Rudolf Steiner, in his spiritual-scientific commentary on this principal prayer of Christianity, referred to as working in a definitive way above all in human social relationships. It is, moreover, in the social sphere that all three of the principal qualities of true forgiveness described in the first part of this chapter are manifested with particular intensity, bringing health to the life of the social organism and permeating it with new powers.

In the first place there is the element of knowledge (insight) that is contained in forgiveness; it is necessary to be wholly conscious of why it is that another person who has committed an evil deed to a certain extent always does so unfreely, submitting himself to the lower forces of his nature—inasmuch as even in the most insignificant evil movement of his soul his will immediately loses its freedom, becoming a blind instrument of the egoistic impulses of his lower ego. For man is free only when his will proceeds from, and is guided by, his higher ego alone.[127] Thus it is really only possible to forgive by consciously or unconsciously experiencing the higher ego of the other person in its relationship with Christ, in its kinship to the substance of Christ, who—in Rudolf Steiner's words—enters into humanity at the Turning Point of Time 'as a special *Cosmic Spirit Self*'[128] and has since then worked in earthly evolution as the Archetype of the higher ego of every human being. This means that

in every individual who has overcome all the negative influences of
the lower ego through the forces of the higher ego this Archetype
can be found and perceived. This is what the spiritual world indicates to George Ritchie, who at first seeks only a repetition of the
clairvoyant experience of Christ that he had been given: Seek His
further revelation in other people. From the standpoint of
Anthroposophy one could add: through perceiving Him in their
higher egos.

In this sense, to forgive means to experience with full intensity
the fact that a person who commits an evil deed takes upon himself
a considerable degree of guilt with regard to his own higher ego and
to the Spirit Self of Christ that works through it. This stands as an
esoteric truth behind the following words of Christ in the Gospel of
St John: 'One who believes in Him [the Son of God] is not judged,
while one who does not believe is already condemned, because he
has not believed in the *name* [that is, the Spirit Self][129] of the only
begotten Son of God' (3:18). In other words, a person who does not
believe, that is, who has turned away from Christ—and this happens
with every evil deed wrought by man, when the lower ego turns
away from the higher—thereby largely judges himself, depriving
himself of the relationship with his higher ego and with Christ who
works within and through him.

Just such an awareness of the *necessity* for forgiveness in our world
makes us truly *brothers of Christ.* This true forgiveness has, as one of
its chief prerequisites, a real *understanding* and, through this, an—
albeit only partial—sharing in the destiny of the other person (who
may be guilty before us or before others who are, perhaps, not even
known to us), thus making it a part of *one's own destiny* (as was the
case with Bill Cody, who in addition to forgiveness took upon
himself the obligation 'to love every person I came in contact
with'). For 'Christ will [only] acknowledge as His brother someone
who acknowledges the other human being to be his brother.'[130]
These words of Rudolf Steiner stand in direct relationship with the
following words of Christ: 'By all this, all human beings will know
that you are my disciples, if you have love for one another' (John
13:35).

Here we have the true sources of the new social community, the future community of the Holy Spirit, that Spirit who, as the substance of cosmic love, streamed down upon the community of the first Apostles on the day of Pentecost, awakening them from the heavy spiritual sleep under whose influence they had been since Christ's Ascension.[131]

Thus in the path of the Apostles, which in a certain sense is an archetype of the whole further evolution of mankind, we have a prophetic fulfilment of what Rudolf Steiner defined in the words: 'First wisdom, then love, then a wisdom warmed through by love.'[132] In the case of the Apostles this means first the wisdom of initiation, which these closest disciples of Christ brought with them from their previous incarnations and then deepened further through studying the prophetic writings of the ancient Jews about the imminent coming of the Messiah. This wisdom later enabled them to become His disciples. Then in the course of the three years which they spent with Christ, they were increasingly permeated by His love as a cosmic power, until finally, at Pentecost, they were irradiated by what may be described as a higher synthesis of love and wisdom, as 'wisdom warmed through by love' or the Holy Spirit, who comes to revelation within man as his Spirit Self.

Irradiated by such a Spirit of *cognitive love*, man is enabled to lay the foundation of a new social community on Earth resting upon true brotherhood; a community where he experiences himself as a member of the living organism of humanity, in constant awareness of his full *responsibility* for its destiny and for everything that takes place within it.[133] Such a relationship with everything that exists and a responsibility for all that takes place in the world is what man feels as a result of the awakening of the higher ego or Spirit Self within his being. On the other hand, it is precisely in our fifth post-Atlantean epoch, in connection with the development of the consciousness soul among mankind, that very powerful antisocial, divergent impulses are also entering into man. Rudolf Steiner characterizes the opposition of these forces in the following way: 'The Spirit Self will work socially with the same strength that the consciousness soul works antisocially in the course of its evolution. Thus one can say: In this epoch [the fifth] man develops an antisocial element out of the innermost impulses of his soul, but behind all this a spiritual-social element is at work. And this spiritual-social element which is at work behind the scenes will become fully manifest when the light of the Spirit Self dawns in the sixth post-Atlantean period.'[134]

In these words we have a direct indication of the highly important *threshold* which mankind is crossing from our time onwards, the threshold lying between the highest soul members and the lowest spiritual members of man's being.[135] And only to the extent that this threshold is gradually surmounted by humanity will a true spiritual brotherhood—a sign of the approaching sixth cultural epoch—increasingly become a reality in its midst.[136] This is why it is called in the Book of Revelation the 'community of Philadelphia', that is, the community of 'brotherly love'.

However, in the sixth epoch mankind will not simply be a society of fraternally united human beings but will in the deepest sense of the word be a *karmic community*. Rudolf Steiner characterizes a community of this kind in the penultimate lecture of the cycle *The Gospel of St Matthew.*[137] 'Man's individual karma must be united with the karma of communities.' And: 'Karma can be interrelated in such a way that the community can help to bear the karma of the individual.' In a concrete sense this will come about in such a way that if a certain person belonging to such a community (and in the sixth epoch that will include a significant part of humanity—all those who belong to the 'race of the good')[138] were to commit an evil deed, it would be possible to find in the community 'another person who says: "I shall help you bear your karma!" Karma must be fulfilled [that is, the consequences of the deed must be borne and redeemed by the person who has performed it] but the other can help him.' And this can be done by either one or several members of such a community, or else by the community as a whole. In the latter case the whole community will, as it were, say to him: 'You as an individual have acted wrongly, but we are intervening on your behalf! We shall take on what will lead to the adjustment of karma.'

It follows that such an endeavour of a community with regard to one or another of its members will gradually establish a completely new karma among mankind. In the following words, Rudolf Steiner goes on to describe this process in its broad outline: 'Thus through the threads of individual karma being woven into the karma of the whole community a web is spun. And through what Christ has brought down from the spiritual heights, this web is to bear the character of a reflection of the order that prevails in heaven, that is, the karma of the individual is united with the karma of the whole in accordance with the order that prevails in the spiritual world, not in a random fashion but in such a way that the organism of the community becomes a reflection of the order that prevails in heaven.'* In other words, what is being spoken of here is a direct penetration into human karmic relationships of that 'power of the Sun and the cosmos', which 'Christ has brought down from the spiritual heights' and which, working further on the Earth in human individuals and in their communities, is uniquely capable of bringing the karma of humanity into order, that is, of making it a reflection of 'the order that prevails in the spiritual world', that spiritual world whence the Christ Himself descended to Earth at the Turning Point of Time.

In Rudolf Steiner's words, this will be 'the founding of the humanity of the future, a humanity based upon the ego-nature in man', when the whole of mankind—provided, that is, that it lives up to the challenges of its evolution—will be able to join together in a new community, founded upon a full, higher development of the true nature of a human ego that is wholly permeated by the forces of the higher ego or Spirit Self.

Then Christ Himself will be able to work all the more directly within such a community as its new higher group ego. For 'the Christ-impulse can be the same throughout the whole of mankind and yet be a personal affair for every individual.'[139] Thus in a community of this kind the social affiliation to Christ will be able to be combined with total individual freedom and with a very full

---

* This is another aspect of the process described in chapter VI, 2. For wherever breaches occur—through forgiveness—in the web of karmic necessity, this is precisely where the foundation arises for the new Christ (Sun) karma, which is a reflection of the order that prevails in heaven.

development of all the inner qualities and creative possibilities of each individual personality. And the path which leads to the fulfilment of this high ideal will be inseparable from that spiritual development which we have already described in chapter V and whose beginning is marked by tolerance and, in particular, by the capacity for forgiveness. Rudolf Steiner refers to this in such a way that, in the following words, he anticipates the description which we have already quoted of the gradual arising among mankind of a new karmic web permeated by the Christ-impulse: 'If one understands "binding" and "loosening" in this way, one would with every act of *forgiveness* of sins have to consider the obligation which this entails on the part of the community.' When we were considering the story of Bill Cody, we spoke about the very definite 'obligation' which an association of human beings in the first instance takes upon itself with regard to one of its members who has committed a misdeed—namely, that it is a sacrificial giving to the world of the same measure of forces of goodness and love as had been taken away from it by the wrongful action.

This will be the beginning of the fulfilment of what the Apostle Paul refers to as the only 'law of Christ': 'Bear one another's burdens, and so fulfil the law of Christ' (Galatians 6:2). By these words is meant, of course, not outward help or the bearing of an outward 'burden' but help in the sphere of karma such as leads to taking upon oneself the karma of another person or even of a group of people.

★

What has been characterized here as an ideal of the future, the first stage in the fulfilment of which is, within the context of humanity as a whole, attainable only in the sixth epoch, must be prepared *already in our time* by those who are endeavouring to unite in the General Anthroposophical Society. For it is precisely in the period of his rulership over earthly evolution that Michael, in his capacity of Time Spirit and at the behest of Christ as His countenance, wants to endow human beings with a new spiritual strength which can enable them consciously to aspire towards bringing order to karma:

'But how is it, then, that there are also forces which work in such a way that people today find their way together under purely spiritual principles when in the ordinary everyday world they are otherwise complete strangers to one another? In what do the forces consist which lead people to find one another? They consist in that through the onset of the rulership of Michael, through the Michael age in which we live, with the entry of Michael into his earthly rulership ... the power which is to restore order to the karma of those who have followed him is introduced by Michael. Thus we may ask: What unites the members of the Anthroposophical Society? It is that they are to bring order again into their karma.'[140]

This also explains the particular significance of developing the capacity of forgiveness among anthroposophists, for if it is not developed the Anthroposophical Society will never be able fully to become what it was to become after the Christmas Conference: a domain of conscious work on the part of spiritually striving human beings to bring order to karma. In an occult sense this means that after the Christmas Conference the work of overcoming the old Moon karma and creating the new Sun karma was to be begun on a large scale within the newly founded General Anthroposophical Society.

Moon karma is that which every human being leaves behind after death in the Moon-sphere that is in immediate proximity to the Earth (hence its name) in order again to unite with it immediately before his new incarnation on Earth.[141] Also connected with this karma are the consequences of his evil deeds, thoughts and feelings in all his previous incarnations. It is for this reason that when in his life after death man enters the Sun-sphere, where evil cannot exist, he must leave his karma behind—in the Moon-sphere. Sun karma, on the other hand, is that which man works upon after death together with the beings of the higher Hierarchies in the Sun-sphere (on Devachan). However, in contrast to Moon karma, which in the course of a human being's new birth enters with him into earthly life as an iron necessity, Sun karma can be fulfilled by man on Earth only in total freedom, upon the foundation of his own spiritual exertions.

For this reason, it was their *Sun karma*, which consisted in their

common participation in a supersensible School of Michael in the
Sun-sphere between the fifteenth and the seventeenth centuries,
that was placed before the members of the Anthroposophical
Society after the Christmas Conference; because only through an
ever more conscious relationship to this common cosmic past of all
true anthroposophists can a power be generated which leads to the
gradual overcoming of the Moon karma (or the karma of the lower
ego) which divides and hampers the whole of evolution, and to the
incarnation (realization) on Earth—and above all in the Anthroposophical Society itself—of the Sun karma (or the karma of the
higher ego) which unites them. And its realization on the Earth, as a
direct fulfilment of the impulse of Michael-Christ in our time, will
serve as a foundation for that community of the spirit referred to
above which in the sixth epoch is to form the good part of
humanity.

If this Sun karma is to be fulfilled on Earth within the General
Anthroposophical Society, there is in the first place a need for the
preservation and the general strengthening of what was given to it
by Rudolf Steiner at the Christmas Conference in the form of the
'dodecahedral Foundation Stone of love',[142] of the new spiritual-
moral substance of which Marie Steiner writes in her 'Appeal for
Reconciliation' of 1942; because this *moral substance* is what is
needed in order to be able truly to work upon bringing order to
karma. Marie Steiner writes in this connection: 'And yet miracles
can still happen. They happen when the moral substance is of such
strength that it can make a miracle possible. What can we do to
rescue our moral substance? We can forgive! Everyone can forgive
what lies within him to forgive.'

These words have indeed not lost their urgency even to this day.
For with every act of true forgiveness is associated a sacrifice, the
sacrificial outpouring of the highest moral substance of the soul into
the world; and this leads to the establishing in the world of that Sun
karma which overcomes the Moon karma, the Sun karma which is
intended to be the true esoteric content of the Anthroposophical
Society since the Christmas Conference and of which—albeit in
different words—Marie Steiner speaks in her 'Appeal'.[143]

To conclude this chapter, a further observation of Rudolf

Steiner's will be cited which testifies to the significance of true *brotherhood* as the social foundation for all anthroposophical work, a quality which, as we have seen, is attainable only through the development of a real capacity for forgiveness: 'Anthroposophy demands as an essential quality a truly human brotherliness which extends into the deepest regions of the soul. In other cases one can say: brotherliness is a precept. In the case of Anthroposophy one must say: it will grow only upon the foundation of brotherliness, it cannot grow except out of brotherliness, such as arises where the individual *gives* to the other what he has and what he can.'[144] By the need to 'give' to the other what '[one] has and what [one] can' that is spoken of here, it is necessary to understand not only knowledge or spiritual experience but also that spiritual-moral substance which is indicated by the genius of the German language in the word 'ver*geben*'.

Only when through such a continual 'giving' has the Anthroposophical Society, and all the branches and working groups of which it is composed, made the principle of brotherhood an actuality in its midst will the following words of the modern spiritual researcher become a reality: 'And through the fact that we join together, that we unite in *brotherly* associations in order to pursue our spiritual science, we are preparing what is to permeate the sixth post-Atlantean cultural period as culture, as civilization . . . The work that we are doing in our *brotherly* working groups streams up towards the growing forces that have been prepared for the Spirit Self.'[145]

Thus already in our time the Anthroposophical Society is called to prepare the spiritual culture of the sixth post-Atlantean epoch; it is called to pioneer the path leading to the future descent of the Spirit Self to humanity and to the new social form that will be founded upon it.

VII

The Nature of Forgiveness and the Sevenfold
Manichaean Initiation

Three problems are especially characteristic for the modern epoch:
the problem of the ego, the social problem, and the problem of evil.
The relationship of the first two of these to forgiveness has already
been considered at some length in the present work. Now it is
necessary to turn to the last and perhaps the most difficult of these
problems.

At the end of the fourth lecture of the cycle *From Symptom to
Reality in Modern History*,[146] Rudolf Steiner speaks with particular
intensity about the significance of the problem of evil for, and the
need for a real understanding of it in, our fifth post-Atlantean
epoch. He first refers to how the most characteristic feature of the
fourth, Graeco-Latin, cultural epoch was the experience that every
individual had within his soul, the problem of birth and death. But
what was at that time experienced by human beings in an inward
way has in our fifth epoch become an outward affair. Thus in our
time we are constantly coming up against both large- and small-
scale manifestations of the ceaselessly alternating processes of birth
and death, of coming into being and passing away, everywhere in
the world around us, and especially in social life, in the sphere
where human beings live and work together—this being an influence which extends to the events of human history. In order to
really *understand* these processes one needs to become thoroughly
familiar with the idea of repeated earthly lives, without a knowledge
of which the problem of birth and death will increasingly become a
kind of meaningless nightmare that surrounds us everywhere: 'But
just as man's consciousness of birth and death has passed from an

inner experience to an outer phenomenon, so in the fifth post-Atlantean epoch must he develop within himself something which in the sixth post-Atlantean epoch (i.e. in the fourth millennium) will again be experienced externally. And that something is evil.'[147]

Just as in the fourth cultural epoch mankind as a whole had to pass through an inner encounter with birth and death, so in our fifth epoch must there be an inner experience of the conscious encounter with evil. For both of these truly fundamental experiences of earthly humanity, two central events have been inserted into human evolution which serve to indicate man's true relationship to death, on the one hand, and to evil, on the other. One of these is the Mystery of Golgotha, which took place historically (that is, on the physical plane) at that time when the problem of birth and, especially, of death was the most important problem for mankind. The second event is the supersensible appearance of Christ in the etheric body from the twentieth century onwards, an event which is associated with a kind of renewal of the Mystery of Golgotha, though now not on Earth but in the supersensible world nearest to it. Rudolf Steiner speaks about this as follows: 'Today, when Christ is to appear again in the etheric body, when a kind of Mystery of Golgotha is to be experienced anew, evil has a significance akin to that of birth and death for the fourth post-Atlantean epoch ... . Thus by a strange paradox, mankind is led to a renewed experience of the Mystery of Golgotha in the fifth epoch through the forces of evil. Through the experience of evil it will be possible for the Christ to appear again, just as He appeared in the fourth post-Atlantean epoch through the experience of death.'

How are we to understand these words which at first sound so puzzling: 'Mankind is led to a renewed experience of the Mystery of Golgotha ... through the forces of evil' and also that 'through the experience of evil it will be possible for the Christ to appear again...'? We can find an answer to this question in another of Rudolf Steiner's lectures, one that he had given five and a half years previously. There he describes how, beginning especially from the sixteenth century, an ever-increasing number of human souls have entered the spiritual world through the gates of death bearing the purely materialistic impulses which they have assimilated on Earth, the effect of which in the spiritual world nearest to the Earth has been like an ever-intensifying darkening of the Sun. This process reached its culmination in the second half of the nineteenth century, a time which Rudolf Steiner often characterized as the highest point in the evolution of materialism in the entire historical evolution of mankind. Thus by the last third of the nineteenth century a ring-shaped region of spiritual darkness, encircling the Earth, had formed in the spiritual world nearest to the Earth, as a result of whose presence there was a real danger that the dark age of the Kali Yuga, which was supposed to end in 1899, might be artificially extended into the age of the light epoch. In other words, the mighty stream of new spiritual impulses which was to flow into humanity from the twentieth century onwards could have been held back by this ring of spiritual darkness around the Earth. The result of this would have been that the new 'Christ-consciousness', together with the new clairvoyant faculties associated with it, would not have been able to evolve within humanity at the necessary time.

In order to prevent this happening, that mighty event took place in the spiritual world nearest to the Earth in the last third of the nineteenth century which Rudolf Steiner calls the supersensible 'repetition of the Mystery of Golgotha', and this rescued humanity from this danger: 'The seeds of earthly materialism, which since the sixteenth century had been borne into the spiritual world in ever greater measure by the souls passing through the gate of death and which were bringing ever more darkness in their wake, formed the "black sphere of materialism". This black sphere was received by Christ into His Being—*in the sense of the Manichaean principle*—in order that He might transform it ... This sacrifice of Christ in the nineteenth century is comparable with the sacrifice on the physical plane in the Mystery of Golgotha and can be described as the second Crucifixion of Christ on the etheric plane ... Christ has now been crucified once physically, in the physical world at the beginning of our era, and a second time spiritually, in the nineteenth century, in the way described above. It could be said that mankind experienced the resurrection of His body in that former time and will experience the resurrection of His consciousness from the twentieth century onwards.' Thus the Christ-consciousness can be united with the earthly consciousness of people from the twentieth century onwards: 'Christ's life will from the twentieth century onwards be felt more and more as a direct personal experience in the souls of human beings.'[148]

Thus as a result of this deed of Christ, which has its origin in the evil wrought by mankind and in the introduction of its consequences into the spiritual world, a path opens up before the whole of humanity, beginning from the twentieth century, towards a completely new experience of His Being as the only firm foundation of earthly evolution in the future.

The principal task of our epoch is that the forces of evil must enter into the inner world of human beings. But they must enter into it not in order to compel or entice human beings to engage in evil deeds but in order that man might become able to develop within himself a true spiritual life: 'Man must assimilate these forces of evil which exert their authority in the universe. By so doing, he implants in his being the seeds which enable him to experience the life of the spirit through the consciousness-soul.'[149]

However, the question as to whether such a (from a higher point of view) necessary experience of the principle of evil within human beings[150] will contribute towards the advancement or the destruction of humanity will depend upon people's efforts to develop within themselves the new 'Christ-consciousness' through which they may find the way to a clairvoyant experience of the Etheric Christ. The means for such a development are given in modern spiritual science—the spiritual language which alone can enable mankind today to turn consciously to the Etheric Christ.[151]

Thus in the repetition of the Mystery of Golgotha, which is the supersensible source of Christ's appearance to human beings in the etheric sphere for all ages to come (if they will only seek this through modern spiritual science), there is given not only a means of spiritual orientation but also an actual spiritual *power* with whose help the necessary receiving of evil into oneself can be translated into a process of arousing an entirely new capacity of perceiving 'the Spirit who proceeds from the universe', in order that, through this Spirit permeating the whole of modern culture, it may be spiritualized: 'If man did not receive into himself these inclinations towards evil ... he would not be able to unfold the impulse from out of his consciousness soul to reach out towards the Spirit who must henceforth fructify the whole sphere of cultural life if it is not to perish—that is, the Spirit who proceeds from the universe.'[152]

This 'Spirit who proceeds from the universe' is the spirit-bearer of that new revelation which must now, with the ending of Kali Yuga, flow into humanity—the possibility for which was brought about by Christ through His having transformed the 'black sphere of materialism' around the Earth.

In the above-quoted words of Rudolf Steiner about the repetition of the Mystery of Golgotha, there is a particular significance in the indication that it took place 'in the sense of the Manichaean principle'. Hence we have here a *higher archetype* of the fundamental mission of Manichaeism amongst mankind—not a repudiation of, or a running away from, evil but, in contrast, a total 'receiving' of evil 'into oneself' and then its 'transformation' into good by the forces which spring from the new clairvoyant experience of Christ.

Here we touch upon a deep occult mystery, where the two processes under consideration—the transformation of the laws of karma through true forgiveness and the transmutation of the forces of objective evil into good through the repetition of the Mystery of Golgotha in the etheric world—are united.

According to Rudolf Steiner, the egoistic desires and passions aroused in man by luciferic beings were countered by the higher powers through suffering and illness, and the cold intellectual evil of Ahriman was kept within bounds by means of the iron laws of karma.[153] This means that when a person works out of powers of forgiveness on the transformation of karma, he is repeating on a microcosmic scale what Christ accomplished in the supersensible worlds when He passed through the etheric Mystery of Golgotha and was thereby enabled to influence—in a way different from before—the process as to how humanity lives out its earthly karma, in that He entered into a relationship to this karma of which Rudolf Steiner says that 'Christ became the Lord of Karma'.

★

We have already (in chapter V) spoken at some length of the relationship that exists between the process of forgiveness and the new capacity of beholding Christ in the etheric sphere. Now this relationship must be considered from a somewhat different point of view, namely, from the standpoint of the problem of evil and its transformation into good in the true Manichaean Mysteries. According to Rudolf Steiner, these Mysteries cannot as yet be fully revealed in our time to humanity. Hence it is possible to say only a little about them in the present work. For the purposes of our theme, it is necessary to refer to one process in particular which may be called 'moral breathing'.

In order that we may best understand its nature, let us consider for a moment man's ordinary breathing process. What happens when we breathe? Firstly, by means of the breath we take into our organism from the world around us, oxygen is saturated with life-forces, and then, as we breathe out, we give back to it carbon dioxide, the bearer of death-forces which kill everything that lives. Thus one can say that man is fashioned in such a way that he continually inhales life and exhales death. The opposite process takes place in plants. This is why the contrast between plant and man plays so essential a part in the fundamental Rosicrucian meditation.[154]

However in the future, which begins already in our epoch, man will—as a result of his progress on the path of inner development which has been made accessible to him by the science of initiation—be able gradually to acquire the faculty of inhaling carbon dioxide in full consciousness and exhaling oxygen. To a very small, barely perceptible, degree, this happens with intense meditative work. But in the sixth cultural epoch this process of spiritualizing the breathing will intensify to such a degree that it will to a certain extent be possible to speak about the very first stages in overcoming the forces of death in human evolution.[155]

In a similar way, man will be able in future to unfold within himself a different, more inward, faculty—namely, one of 'moral breathing'. He will be able to 'inhale' evil and then 'exhale' good, in the same way that he now learns in meditation to convert carbon dioxide back into oxygen.[156] This process of inwardly transforming evil into good through 'moral breathing'—the archetype of which is the 'repeated Mystery of Golgotha'—will be developed amongst mankind over the course of the sixth cultural epoch; while in the seventh, at the height of the 'War of All against All', a start will be made in the gradual overcoming of evil, which will in the fullest sense be the task of the next (sixth) *great* period[157] of earthly evolution, which will witness the highest flowering and the widest diffusion on Earth of the Manichaean Mysteries.

Thus in the lecture of 11 November 1904, the theme of which is Manicheism, Rudolf Steiner speaks of how this esoteric stream founded by Manes, or Mani, in the third century of the Christian era was 'an even more important spiritual stream than Rosicrucianism'. And then he continues: 'Mani's intention is to create a spiritual stream which goes beyond the Rosicrucian stream, which leads further than Rosicrucianism. This stream of Mani will flow over to the Sixth Root Race, which has been in preparation since the founding of Christianity.'[158] In the same lecture, Rudolf Steiner formulates the essential task of this stream as follows: 'The Sixth Root Race will have the task of drawing evil back as far as it can into the continuing stream of evolution through gentleness. Then a spiritual stream will have been born which does not oppose evil, even when it appears in the world in its most demonic form,' and which has the consciousness '. . . that evil must be included again in evolution and that it shall be overcome not by strife but solely through gentleness. It is the task of the Manichaean spiritual stream to make vigorous efforts to prepare for this.'

Of course, when the Manichaean Mysteries gradually begin to be fully manifested amongst mankind from the seventh epoch onwards, this process of 'moral breathing' will bear a *magical character*. Rudolf Steiner refers to this when he speaks of how representatives of the 'good race will [for the purpose of turning towards the good those people who have succumbed to the forces of evil and who thereby form the "evil race"] understand how to set the occult forces in motion'.[159]

However, it is possible to prepare oneself for these future tasks of 'good humanity' already in our time. And the path to this is that of tolerance and *forgiveness*. Especially in the latter, we have real seeds of that process of 'moral breathing' which has been spoken of. For in every case where we have been subjected to evil we receive or, one could also say, spiritually 'inhale' it into ourselves in such a way that its consequences continue to work within our soul; while in an act of true forgiveness we firstly—through overcoming ourselves— transform these consequences into good and then send this good back into the world, spiritually 'exhaling' it, as it were, in order to give back to the world as much goodness and love as was taken from it as a result of the wrongful action.

In his lecture on 'Manichaeism', Rudolf Steiner particularly singles out that soul quality which in the German language is referred to as *Milde* [kindness, gentleness][160] as the most effective moral instrument to enable the followers of Manes to wage the battle with the evil in earthly evolution. This word is not merely in its meaning but also through its etymological roots related to the word 'forgiveness' (*Verzeihen*). Even in ordinary life we quite naturally presuppose that a person to whose character we may apply the word 'mild' (gentle) is most likely to have a considerable capacity for forgiveness. (Moreover, gentleness in the truly Man-ichaean sense is by no means a sign of soul weakness but a power of the mightiest kind, fully capable of transforming man's etheric body, as was the case, for example, with Bill Cody.)

Etymologically, the German word *mild* derives from the old High German *milt*, which means 'good', 'gracious', and in its origin goes back to the Ancient Indian *mardhati*, which means 'forgets', 'leaves in the lurch'. In other words, we have here an evolution brought about by the genius of language itself from 'forgetting' to 'goodness' and 'grace'; and it is such a 'bounteous forgetting' which arises in the human soul in the process of 'forgiveness' (*Verzeihen*), a word which derives from *verzichten*, which is in its turn associated with the notion of voluntary renunciation and, in a deeper sense, of voluntary forgetting.

On the other hand, the word *Milde* is related to that virtue which Parsifal had to develop on the path towards his initiation.[161] Wolfram von Eschenbach uses the word *saelde* to refer to it, a word which is related to the Gothic *selei*, meaning 'goodness, gentleness', and also to the Anglo-Saxon *sǣlig*—'fortunate', 'good', 'blessed' ('highly favoured', 'blissfully happy').

Developing within oneself *saelde* means, therefore, creating the conditions in one's soul which can enable the cosmic Spirit to descend into one's ego as the Spirit Self, that is, that Spirit with whom Christ prophetically endows His Apostles when He sends them out into the world to *forgive* people in His *name* and remit their sins.[162] Rudolf Steiner defines the word *saelde* in the same sense as the 'life ... which pours forth spiritual knowledge over the consciousness soul' and through which alone '... human soul-development [can] make a really fruitful transition from the fifth epoch to the sixth.'[163]

Thus in the words *Milde* and *saelde* in their relationship to the principle of forgiveness we may discern the direction of the development which will in future lead to the founding of the true Manichaean Mysteries among mankind.

★

In chapter V we described a path which is a particular metamorphosis of the sevenfold Rosicrucian Path. Its principal stages were: tolerance, forgiveness, taking upon oneself the karma of individual people or of a whole society, participating in bearing the karma of humanity, and, finally, the gradual redeeming of the beings of opposition. Now, after all that has been said in the present chapter, this path can with justice be called a *Manichaean* path, although we ought not to identify it directly with the Manichaean Mysteries of the far future, which will bear a magical character. Nevertheless, this path leads to them and is preparing their future revelation already in our time, that is, a manifestation not only in the inner realm of knowing but, even beyond the realm of feeling, in the realm of will, the realm of moral intuition.

In chapter V it was said that the path which we have designated as the Manichaean is 'the way to the Christ through thinking'. In a similar way the modern Christian-Rosicrucian path can be designated as 'the way to the Christ through willing'. Its beginning and foundation—in Rudolf Steiner's words—is the *new idealism* which man consciously develops within himself,[164] without which it is impossible rightly to traverse the first stage of the Rosicrucian path, the stage of the *study* of spiritual science, which has its origin in a direct investigation of the supersensible world.

Both paths—the Rosicrucian and the Manichaean—are in their inner nature very close to one another. They can be compared with the two ascending serpents around the Mercury staff (the Caduceus). Indeed, all the principal elements of the one can be found in the other and vice versa. Their difference consists, rather, in a certain inner emphasis and in their different points of departure.

The Christian-Rosicrucian path is from the outset concerned with *introducing the impulse of will into the sphere of knowledge*. This takes place at the following levels: study, and the imaginative, inspirative, intuitive and three further stages of knowledge.

The Manichaean path, on the other hand, begins with tolerance, that is, with *bringing thinking* (understanding) *into the*—for ordinary consciousness *initially dark*—*realm of the will*; and this engendering of consciousness within the impulses of the will enables an immediate beginning to be made with the 'creating of the outward social form', 'the outward form of life'[165] in which all these new and ever higher revelations of Christ that have been spoken of in the present work will come to be perceived in the future. Rudolf Steiner says in this connection: 'This is what Manichaeism is striving for. It is not so much a question of cultivating the inner life [in the sense of knowledge], for life will flow onwards through other channels—but rather of cultivating the outward form of life.' And those soul-forces upon whose foundation this 'form of life'—as a social entity—is to be established are essentially those that we have characterized as tolerance, forgiveness and the endeavour to take upon oneself the karma of others.

The inner connection and at the same time the difference between the points of departure of the two spiritual paths can be discerned with particular clarity in the example of 'moral breathing' described above. As was shown, the transformation process of evil into good through 'moral breathing' has its archetype in the 'second Mystery of Golgotha', in the course of which Christ 'inhaled' into His Being in the spiritual world adjacent to the Earth all the darkness of the materialistic thoughts of the materialistically inclined souls of the nineteenth century which had passed through the gate of death, and 'exhaled' spiritual light, which awakens within man a new Christ-consciousness, evokes spiritual thoughts and will lead man in future to a conscious experience of the Etheric Christ.[166]

Something similar, albeit initially only in a very small way, happens through working with Anthroposophy. For man is today, in that he is born into and lives within modern materialistic civilization, whether he wishes or not, continually forced to 'breathe into' his soul the materialistic thoughts, ideas, feelings and will-impulses that it calls forth. And if nothing else intervenes, the materialistic content of modern civilization works like a poisonous substance which constantly undermines the soul.

Through Anthroposophy, on the other hand, it is possible to oppose this destructive process by means of an inner activity of the soul, everywhere to seek the spirit in matter. Initially, this takes place on the plane of thought, through the results of anthroposophical spiritual research being assimilated. The consequence of this is that individuals who had formerly always 'inhaled' the materialistic conceptions of modern civilization learn in ever-growing measure to 'exhale' the spiritual thoughts of modern spiritual science into this civilization and to deepen and extend this process to the sphere of feeling and finally to that of concrete action, which then results in the renewal of practically all realms of human life and activity—art, science (Goetheanism), education, agriculture, medicine, banking, the social order and so on—out of the impulses of the spirit. For in that man endeavours consistently—through Anthroposophy—to *think* spiritually in all the areas of modern materialistic civilization and then to make its transforming impulses a reality, he is already acting within the supersensible stream of forces which proceeds from the etheric Mystery of Golgotha. Significantly Rudolf Steiner characterized Anthroposophy as the spiritual 'language' in which present-day humanity can turn directly to the Etheric Christ.[167]

A particularly significant example of this 'breathing' process in the cognitive sphere can be found in Rudolf Steiner's life, when he wholly assimilated the thoroughly materialistic 'anthropology' of Ernst Haeckel and, after having inwardly transformed it by means of modern Christian-Rosicrucian initiation, raised it up into the spiritual world to the Gods, to Michael, and then received it back as the deeply spiritual content of his book *Occult Science*. He describes this process as follows: 'If today ... you study the ideas of Haeckel, with all their materialism, and at the same time permeate yourselves with the methods of cognition presented in *Knowledge of the Higher Worlds* ... you will learn all that can be learned through modern natural science and then offer it up to the Gods—and you will arrive at what is related about evolution in my book *Occult Science*.[168]

As one reads these words, one must be clear that this process—in its modern form—would be completely impossible without the second Mystery of Golgotha. In this sense, Rudolf Steiner—enacting it as he did *in full consciousness*—was working wholly out of these forces. In the spiritual schools of the Rosicrucians such attempts were indeed made in recent times, though, as Rudolf Steiner indicates in the lecture quoted, even so high an initiate as Christian Rosenkreutz was only able to achieve this in a dulled (clairvoyant) state of consciousness *before* the second Mystery of Golgotha.[169] Here the Rosicrucian path crosses the Manichaean. The difference is simply that the latter, as we have seen, does not have its application in the cognitive element but in the will element, which is primarily directed towards the transformation of evil into good in the *moral sphere*, and this means that this path too—in its present form—has its origin in the repetition of the Mystery of Golgotha.

Following this path *in full consciousness* will, to be sure, only become possible from our time onwards, even though the qualities of gentleness, tolerance, readiness for sacrifice, and the capacity for forgiveness which are seminal for true Manichaean initiation were originally common to all the spiritual streams which to one degree or another were under its influence, as, for example, the streams of the Albigenses, Waldenses, Cathars, Bulgarian Bogomils and others. Their chief aspiration was not primarily to search for knowledge but to establish communities where all the original Gospel precepts might find their fulfilment and above all those which, in their opinion, were more permeated with a true Manichaean spirit. Among these may be numbered in particular the injunctions from the Gospel about 'non-resistance to evil [violence]', 'returning good for evil', 'loving one's enemies' and finally the sayings of Christ about 'forgiveness'.[170] With all the more cruelty were they persecuted by the official Roman Catholic Church, an impulse which may be traced back to the conflict between the Church Father Augustine and the Manichaean bishop Faustus. Rudolf Steiner speaks about this as follows: 'Two polar opposites confront one another, Faustus and Augustine: Augustine, who based his work on the Church, on the form belonging to his day, and Faustus, who strives to prepare in man a sense for the form of the future. That is the contrast which developed in the third and fourth centuries AD. It is still present and finds expression in the struggle of the Catholic Church against the Knights Templar, the Rosicrucians, Albigenses, Cathars and so on.'[171]

By subjecting these streams to cruel persecutions, which in the majority of cases ended with their complete physical annihilation, the Roman Catholic Church manifested with particular intensity features diametrically opposed not only to the sects enumerated above but also to the very spirit of Christianity. It will suffice here to mention one very well-known example.

After the declaration by Pope Innocent III in 1209 of a 'crusade' against the 'Albigensian heresy', a Catholic army—accompanied by the Papal Legate, Abbot Arnaud—Amalric—came in that same year to the town of Béziers, which lies in the South of France, with the object of wiping out all the 'heretics' gathered there. Before the capture of the town—only a part of whose inhabitants were Albigenses, the remainder being adherents of orthodox Catholicism— the Papal Legate was asked how the Catholics could be distinguished from the 'heretics'. He answered: 'Tuez les tous, Dieux reconnaîtra les siens' ('Kill them all, God will recognize His own'). After this there followed a terrible battle as a result of which practically all the inhabitants of the town were wiped out, and the town itself was destroyed and burnt to the ground. In the church of St Magdalen alone—where many of the town's inhabitants had sought refuge—approximately seven thousand people were killed on that day, including a large number of children, women and old people.[172]

Nevertheless, not even the physical annihilation of the Cathars

and Albigenses in the thirteenth and of the Templars in the fourteenth century was able to stifle the Manichaean spiritual impulse
that stood behind them: 'They are all eliminated from the physical
plane, but their inner spirit continues to be active.'[173] This inner
spirit now, however, begins to work esoterically. For the fruit of the
high council of the leading Christian initiates of the West summoned by Manes in the fourth century was the founding shortly
after 1250, wholly unbeknown to the outer world, of the Rosicrucian stream, which absorbed much of Manichaean wisdom and
also the wisdom of the Grail Mysteries (which originated in the
eighth/ninth centuries).[174] The spiritual relationship and inner
succession of these three principal streams of esoteric Christianity
was made an outward reality through the fact that the high individuality of Manes not only participated personally in the further
evolution of the Grail Mysteries in the ninth century but was over
the centuries one of the leading Masters in the Rosicrucian Mysteries.[175]

From this it becomes clear that a large part of Manichaean occult
knowledge has also been inherited by spiritual science or Anthroposophy, which represents the *modern form* of Christian esotericism
as it originally emerged in the Grail Mysteries (of which the
Rosicrucian stream became the continuation at the threshold of the
modern age).

And yet Rudolf Steiner speaks remarkably little in his numerous
lectures about the Manichaean *Mysteries* themselves or about the
path of initiation leading to them. This is for the same reason that he
speaks so little about forgiveness—namely, that even the first stages
of this spiritual path are so very difficult for modern man. He
indicates this in the eighth lecture of the cycle on the 'Apocalypse':
'Although at the present day this principle of Manes has had to step
very much into the background because there is little understanding
for spiritual work, this wonderful and lofty Manichaean principle
will win more and more pupils the nearer we approach an understanding of spiritual life.'[176]

These words of the founder of Anthroposophy enable us to feel
the extent to which the Manichaean path—at any rate in its initial
stages—will by the end of our century have become a vital necessity

for the Anthroposophical Society, inasmuch as it has as its central task not only that of 'approaching an understanding of the spiritual life' but of cultivating it in modern civilization. Thus on this path there is a need to develop quite definite inner qualities, an endeavour that will especially be demanded of the Anthroposophical Society as mankind makes the transition to the third millennium of the Christian era—provided that the Anthroposophical Society itself really tries to fulfil the high spiritual tasks placed before it by its founder.

In our time—and this tendency will grow ever stronger in the immediate future—the impulses of evil have become so powerful throughout earthly evolution that inner powers reaching far beyond what is ordinarily called good or moral will have to be found if mankind is to be able to cope with them. What is particularly—and immediately—necessary in this connection is the mastering of that spiritual process which has been defined as 'moral breathing', the beginning of which is forgiveness.

★

The immediate relevance of the theme of forgiveness for our time derives primarily from its connection—as we have described it—with the new appearance of Christ in the etheric sphere. Thus to a certain extent we can say: if there have as yet been so few who have been honoured with a real clairvoyant experience of the Etheric Christ, this is by no means unconnected with the fact that the forces of forgiveness—and, hence, the Manichaean impulse that stands behind them—have hitherto not been developed with sufficient strength among mankind. And on the other hand, if in forgiveness we have a highly important condition for beholding the Etheric Christ, who from our time onwards (and over the course of the next three millennia) is gradually becoming the Lord of Karma,[177] it follows that anthroposophists—who have been given the keys of higher knowledge, and, with them, the possibility of *conscious* work in the field of karma—must make particular efforts to develop these three qualities of tolerance, forgiveness, and bearing another person's karma. For only through the presence of these three truly

Manichaean faculties, and the 'moral substance' that is founded upon them, will the Anthroposophical Society acquire the inner right to lead humanity as a whole to the resolution of the chief problems of the modern epoch: the problem of the ego, the social problem and the problem of evil.

VIII

The Manichaean Impulse in the Life of Rudolf Steiner

Even a cursory familiarity with Rudolf Steiner's description of his youth in his autobiography, *The Course of My Life*, makes one aware of the abundance and variety of his acquaintances and the large number of his friendships. At that time Rudolf Steiner appears in the most diverse circles, the participants of which frequently have nothing in common with one another.

Take, for example, his life in Vienna, at the end of the 1880s. There he associates with and befriends the Goethe scholar Karl Julius Schröer, visits the home of the talented poetess Marie Eugenie della Grazie, around whom professors of the faculty of Catholic theology gather regularly. Later, also in Vienna, he becomes acquainted with a small circle of people interested in Theosophy grouped around Marie Lang and, through her, with Rosa Mayreder, around whom there reigns an atmosphere of free thinking and zealous quests for the true place and significance of women in society. And at the same time he has a correspondence and then a personal acquaintance with the philosopher of the unconscious, Edouard von Hartmann.

The circle of Rudolf Steiner's acquaintances widens still further after his move to Weimar. Here it is his associations with the scientist Ernst Haeckel, the philosopher Nietzsche, the literary critic Herman Grimm and the committed anarchist Henry Mackay which come to have a particular significance for him. What striking personalities, though how utterly incompatible their inner convictions! Finally, the outer circle of Rudolf Steiner's acquaintances reaches its culmination in Berlin, where he goes in 1897 as the editor of two magazines and as a member of two societies: the 'Free Literary' and the 'Free Dramatic'. Now the circle of Rudolf Steiner's acquaintances includes almost the entire spectrum of the cultural life of Germany at the time, extending even to the extreme individualism of Max Stirner and to direct contacts with the Berlin working class (from 1899 until 1904 Rudolf Steiner teaches on a variety of subjects in the Liebknecht Workers Training School).

But what was the inner attitude of Rudolf Steiner which enabled him to feel 'at home'[178] among such different people, among thoughts and spiritual streams that were often wholly incompatible? He answers this question himself in the following words: 'But I was never inclined to deny my admiration and interest in what appeared to me as great, even if as regards its content it stood in direct opposition to me. Yes, I would say to myself: such antitheses must be harmonized somehow or other. And that made it possible for me to develop an understanding of what was contrary to my own path as if it was wholly at one with my own inner attitudes.'

This ability to immerse himself with inner understanding in world conceptions wholly foreign to his own, from Catholicism to Marxism, from Goetheanism to anarchism, was not only natural to Rudolf Steiner from his youth but was consistently and consciously nurtured by him as he progressed in inner development, an advancement which was a consequence of his ever deeper immersion in the spiritual world: 'For I felt at home only in the spiritual world which I was beholding, and I could feel equally well "at home" in *every*★ other.'

It was through his original sense of feeling at home in the spiritual world that Rudolf Steiner was able to experience the world conceptions of other people as reflections of one and the same object, though arrived at from various aspects, from different points of view. The *essential nature* of the object was experienced by him in supersensible contemplation, revealing to him the *relative* rightness of even the most alien ideas: 'But one who possesses a world of *direct perception*, such as the spiritual world *must* be, *sees* the justification of the most varied "standpoints".'[179] Thus as he had passed personally

---

★ In all quotations from *The Course of My Life*, the italics are Rudolf Steiner's.

through this experience, Rudolf Steiner was subsequently fully justified in speaking in his anthroposophical lectures about the twelve points of view from which everything should be considered, if a really comprehensive objective judgement is to be made.

The entire relationship of Rudolf Steiner not only to the world conceptions that came towards him but to the *people* who were their bearers was based on this underlying attitude: 'My gift of observation rested on embracing in my perception, in a wholly pure and objective way, what another person stood for. I was anxious to avoid engaging in criticism of what people did, or allowing sympathy or antipathy to influence my relationship to them; I wanted "to let the person work upon me simply as he is".'[180] The relationship expressed in these words of the young Rudolf Steiner to virtually *all* the people that he met can with justice be characterized as being the direct result of his having developed the quality of *tolerance* to a fairly high degree—tolerance not only in a general moral sense but also in a concrete, occult sense. For in Rudolf Steiner's words he 'soon found that such a way of observing the world truly leads into the spiritual world.' Subsequently he designated this path as 'the way to Christ through thinking.'

However, since Rudolf Steiner had from childhood the gift of clairvoyance and thereby lived more intensely in the spiritual world nearest to the Earth than in the surrounding physical world,[181] it was necessary for him to cultivate a further, far higher and more difficult soul quality—namely, the quality of *forgiveness*. The beginning of his conscious nurturing of this quality can be traced back approximately to the period between his eighteenth and twenty-first years (1879–82), when his capacity of penetrating clairvoyantly into the spiritual world had reached the stage which could be described as the first conscious experience of the higher ego, or the 'spiritual individuality' whose life extends beyond the boundaries of birth and death, as much in others as within his own being.[182] In his autobiography, Rudolf Steiner tells of this as follows: 'But I beheld a spiritual world *as reality*. In perfectly clear vision the spiritual individuality of each person was manifest to me. His physical body and his actions in the physical world were merely its outward expression. It united itself with what was handed down as a physical germ from the parents. I followed the dead person on his way into the spiritual world.'[183]

When Rudolf Steiner subsequently tried to describe this in writing to one of his former teachers at his secondary school,* the latter in his answer passed over this subject in complete silence. Rudolf Steiner continues: 'And this is what happened to me always at that time in this matter of my perception of the spiritual world. No one would pay any attention to it.' This continued to be the case in the years that followed: 'At that time [in the mid-eighties] I found no one to whom I would have been able to speak about these perceptions.' This was the source of that intense inner loneliness which was Rudolf Steiner's lot from earliest childhood and which—as he expressed it—heavily 'burdened' his soul: 'In so far as my perceptions of the spiritual were concerned, I was left entirely on my own. I lived in the spiritual world; no one from my circle of acquaintances followed me there. My intercourse consisted of excursions into the worlds of others.'

★

To the suffering inflicted upon Rudolf Steiner by his spiritual isolation should be added the further circumstance that, in immersing himself in the supersensible worlds ever more deeply into the essential nature of the higher ego, he had—on every return to the physical world—to do almost exclusively with people whose consciousness was active only on the plane of the ordinary everyday ego and did not out of itself wish either to know or to hear about the existence and experiences of the higher ego. In other words, with every 'return' from the spiritual world and entry into the earthly world Rudolf Steiner had to experience that polarization and gulf between the higher and the lower ego which was spoken of at some length in chapter IV. And that tormenting dissonance, that unendurable contradiction which arose in every instance of this kind for Rudolf Steiner and ever and again doomed him not only to

* [Translator's footnote] Rudolf Steiner attended a *Realschule*, where emphasis was placed upon science and modern languages (as opposed to the humanities as such).

total loneliness but also to the most intense inner suffering, comparable to an inner scourging which attacked him with every contact with the sphere of the lower ego of those who surrounded him—this contradiction he was able to overcome only through a continual *forgiveness* of the lack of understanding which everywhere surrounded him.

'This was the nature of my "loneliness" in Weimar at that time, where I led so rich a social life. But I did not ascribe to these persons the fact that they condemned me to such loneliness.' In these words from Rudolf Steiner's autobiography, it is this final sentence which is, essentially, a direct indication of the process of forgiveness which he had continually to fulfil from his earliest youth onwards. For without this higher capacity for forgiveness, the life of an initiate in the midst of contemporary—for the most part materialistically inclined—humanity would be simply impossible. (In chapter III, where we considered the example of Christian Rosenkreutz and his relationship to mankind, we have already examined this problem at some length.)

★

Finally, it is also possible to find in the period of Rudolf Steiner's life before he became a spiritual teacher a whole series of acts which correspond to the *third* stage of the path under consideration—participating in the karma of another person, in certain cases even taking upon oneself (albeit only to a small degree) the karma of another person.

Here some examples may be cited. The first two are associated with names already mentioned in this chapter: Nietzsche and Haeckel. In them, Rudolf Steiner was approaching the two most important representatives of the modern world-view. He visited Nietzsche on his sick-bed, became acquainted with Haeckel on the latter's sixtieth birthday, and experienced both in their spiritual essence. And if on the one hand the extreme materialism of Haeckel and the militant anti-Christianism of the later Nietzsche were profoundly alien to his own world-view, wholly rooted as it was in spiritual contemplation, on the other hand the direct experience of the principal impulses of the epoch—as they worked *through* them, albeit in a very one-sided form—enabled him not only to perceive these impulses outwardly but in an occult sense to unite with them even to their karmic foundations, in order thereby to acquire the possibility of transforming them from within and, hence, of building a solid bridge—resting on firm foundations—leading from natural science to a science of the spirit.

Thus in both the cases of Nietzsche and Haeckel, Rudolf Steiner took the decision consciously to unite with their karma in order thereby to acquire the possibility of turning both these directions towards the spirit.[184] For only through a real sharing in their destinies and world-views was he able to acknowledge at first hand the depth of the abyss that confronted humanity as the dark age of the Kali Yuga came to an end, and also to be aware of the need for it to be vanquished in the course of moving towards the new age of light.

His books *Nietzsche, a Battler Against his Age* (1895) and *Haeckel and his Opponents* (1900) were the fruit of his experience. In both works, Rudolf Steiner indicates the epochal and future-orientated aspects that live as a potential in their world-conceptions and which had therefore to be saved for the further evolution of mankind. However, for Rudolf Steiner himself such a participation in their karma made him for many a year—especially in the eyes of his numerous enemies and ill-wishers—a materialistic Haeckelian for some and a nihilistic Nietzschean for others. Despite this, Rudolf Steiner continued to bear this karma until the end of his life, that is, throughout his activity as an occult teacher, endeavouring to illumine and spiritualize it through his *spiritual* science.[185]

A further, and perhaps the most striking, example is the quite special interweaving—from out of the distant karmic past—of the destinies of Rudolf Steiner and his teacher Karl Julius Schröer. As a result of their meeting and the friendship which arose, it became fully clear to Rudolf Steiner that the task of reassimilating and presenting to a wider public at the end of the nineteenth century all the natural-scientific works of Goethe was the central karmic task of Schröer. Moreover, the fulfilment of this task, which would have demanded of the latter the uniting of the fullness of the spiritual Platonism which he bore within his soul with the intellectualism of modern scientific thinking in its spiritualized form, as was the case with Goethe, would have served as the foundation for the entire future edifice of Anthroposophy.[186]

However, this did not happen. Schröer, despite his interest in and love of Goethe, was unable to gain access to his natural-scientific writings. Then Rudolf Steiner took the decision to fulfil this task *for* Schröer, thus taking upon himself part of his karma and, hence, consciously postponing the fulfilment of his own mission for several years. 'I resolved at that time to live Schröer's destiny as my own and relinquish my own path of destiny,'[187] Rudolf Steiner informed Walter Johannes Stein in April 1922 in The Hague.

Similarly in Rudolf Steiner's relationships to the poets Robert Hamerling and Ludwig Jakobowski, and later to their literary legacy, it is possible to sense elements of an inner participation in their karma. This same motif also appears in Rudolf Steiner's private life, especially in his decision to undertake the education of the children of the Specht family in Vienna and of the Eunike family in Weimar.

★

To an even greater degree than this was Rudolf Steiner called upon to develop these three qualities after he joined the Theosophical Society, an event which was the result of a suggestion on the part of the latter to lead its German section.

It is sufficient merely to call clearly to mind the contrast between Rudolf Steiner, the author of the *Philosophy of Freedom*, with its mountain-airlike freshness and clarity that is impregnated with a free and pure spirituality and permeated with the highest spiritual activity, and the passive, dreamily mystical atmosphere which prevailed in the Theosophical Society at that time. Friedrich Rittelmeyer was from the first sharply aware of this heavy, at times simply repulsive, mood, and later described it in his reminiscences about Rudolf Steiner: 'When I went into the room I was surprised at the atmosphere I found there. The audience, for the most part, gave one an impression of strangeness. A certain type of passive sensation-mongering mentality troubled me. Especially when I saw men with long hair, my impulse was to run away. Later on, all these things changed decidedly for the better, when the "theosophical" shells were laid aside and Rudolf Steiner began to attract more and more people of a scientific turn of mind. He certainly suffered a good deal in those earlier years . . .'[188]

A considerable degree of *tolerance* was indeed demanded of Rudolf Steiner in order that he might live and work in such an environment. He referred to this himself at the very beginning of his activity within the orbit of the Theosophical Society: 'Above all I want to be wholly *positive* in whatever I do . . . positive in *every-thing*.'[189] And true positivity presupposes a tolerance for all manifestations of human endeavour in one's surroundings.

An even greater difficulty, however, lay in the fact that the whole Theosophical Society, since the time of its founder H.P. Blavatsky, was orientated solely towards the Eastern wisdom of India and had an arrogant and scornful attitude towards Christianity as a later and, hence, inferior stage in human evolution. All this was, of course, fundamentally alien to Rudolf Steiner. Nonetheless he took the decision in full responsibility to unite his destiny with the Theosophical Society. The reason for this was that at its founding in 1875 it had originally borne a 'western' character, and there was a number of truths in the first great work of Blavatsky, *Isis Unveiled*, which were 'inspired . . . by the great initiates of the West, who are also the initiators of Rosicrucian wisdom.'[190]

Rudolf Steiner's principal task in this connection was to endeavour to restore the Theosophical Movement—which had subsequently succumbed to the one-sided influence and the group interests of the Eastern occultists and had then been given over to spiritualistic experiments—to its spiritual origins and, hence, to its universally human mission. The majority of the earliest of Rudolf Steiner's lecture-cycles testify to this.

Nevertheless, one can only guess the extent of the inner sufferings to which Rudolf Steiner was subjected by his period of association with the Theosophical Society. Thus he described this 'theosophical' period of his activity as a 'martyrdom'.[191] But once having said 'yes', Rudolf Steiner had no intention of leaving the Theosophical Society out of his own will, and considered it to be his duty to go on working within it through making constant efforts to direct its evolution along the right path. The ever-intensifying attacks, and then the campaign of slander openly unleashed by Annie Besant in response to the position which he had adopted on principle in the 'Alcyone' affair (a campaign which ended with his official expulsion from the society), made it impossible for Rudolf Steiner to continue working within it. Thus the fact remains that it was not he himself but the leadership of the society which severed the connection.[192]

All the same, the consequences of the part he played in bearing the karma of the Theosophical Society have had to be borne by the Anthroposophical Movement even to this day. For despite the fact that even within the orbit of the Theosophical Society Rudolf Steiner invariably worked only in an anthroposophical direction, nevertheless—and this is so even in our own time—many people standing outside the movement (and not only its enemies) have continued to confuse the central stream of esoteric Christianity as represented by Anthroposophy with the Eastern-orientated Theosophy of Blavatsky and Besant and, hence, to number Anthroposophy among the 'non-Christian' streams of modern times. Such is the consequence of Rudolf Steiner's participation in the difficult karma of the Theosophical Society, which not only did not take up but even repudiated the only impulse which might have saved it.

What remains so remarkable is the extent to which Rudolf Steiner was able to manifest a capacity for *forgiveness* precisely at the time of his public espousal of Theosophy. For having—by the beginning of the century—won for himself a name and a reputation as a Goetheanist, philosopher, writer, journalist and critic, he had, in becoming a theosophist, in effect to renounce the whole of his past, including almost all his human relationships and acquaintances; the overwhelming majority of his former friends not only did not want to follow him but had not even the wish to maintain their old friendships with him, mostly because they feared that they might 'compromise' themselves by associating with a 'theosophist', 'occultist', 'clairvoyant', or else simply because they did not understand the step that he had taken.

Thus, for example, when Ernst Haeckel returned after a long journey and heard about the step that Rudolf Steiner had taken, he simply recorded in his correspondence that he 'has meanwhile become a theosophist'—and immediately afterwards broke off all relationships with him. And many of his former friends acted in the same way. Nevertheless, despite the inner pain that he was suffering, Rudolf Steiner *forgave* all who turned away from him in this way. Moreover, he later forgave even those who persecuted and slandered him within the Theosophical Society by deliberately spreading, both within the society and beyond its confines, false rumours to the effect that he was a 'pupil of the Jesuits' or a 'German spy'. It is sufficient to read the characterization of Annie Besant which he gives in his autobiography, where he emphasizes her particular virtues and very evident spiritual capacities without any reference whatsoever to the suffering to which he had been subjected.

★

Instances of tolerance and forgiveness can to an ever-increasing degree be found everywhere in Rudolf Steiner's life. In chapter III a number of such examples have already been given: his forgiveness of anthroposophists for the failure of the movement regarding the threefold social order and also of the two *Hochschulkursen* of 1920 and 1921; his forgiveness for the so-called 'Stuttgart system' and, in particular, his continual forgiveness for that slighting attitude to himself personally which was displayed when he was again and again asked for advice which was then not followed—a circumstance which led to growing difficulties with the Anthroposophical Society, and its relationship to the outer world. And despite this, everywhere 'where fallible human beings had been lacking in some respect, he always set everything once more to rights.'[193]

However, there were times when the relationship of the members of the Anthroposophical Society to himself—which sometimes developed into an inner 'opposition'—led him simply to despair. Thus according to Fred Poeppig, at a certain gathering in the Glass House in 1923 Rudolf Steiner 'with a profoundly sad look repeated the following words several times: "Then I am no more than a *quantité négligeable*," and left the room.'[194] And in some cases—also attested by his pupils—he expressed himself even more sharply about the relationship of certain anthroposophists to himself.

Nevertheless, despite the pain and disappointments to which he was subjected, he continued to endure everything and forgive everyone.

Mention should also be made of his constant and—with the passing years—ever-growing awareness of that inner gulf which, despite all Rudolf Steiner's sufferings, invariably continued to exist between what he brought forth in the course of his lectures by way of new wisdom and higher knowledge directly from the spiritual worlds—from those regions lying beyond the threshold whither he ascended ever and again with his higher ego—and for the most part the very ordinary, earthly consciousness of his listeners. This was especially strongly in evidence at the end of his lectures. Rittelmeyer recalls that 'one felt the tragedy of the loneliness of the great man—but whom, nevertheless, one was not able to help. Rudolf Steiner never let one notice a disappointment and bore this burden with a kind patience.'[195] This polarization was manifested even more forcefully in those innumerable cases when, in his tireless efforts to help one or another person, Rudolf Steiner again and again found himself in a situation where '. . . he addressed the best in the other and the meanest part of him responded'. In this formulation of Friedrich Rittelmeyer there is an indication of that problem arising out of life itself of the antithesis and polarization between the higher and the lower ego, a problem which can be solved only through the constant fulfilment of an inner process of forgiveness.

Finally, it is impossible to forget about those sufferings that Rudolf Steiner was caused throughout his life, especially latterly, as a result of the endless attacks, slander and mockery of a large number of outward foes, such as religious fanatics, dogmatic scientists and many, many others. Friedrich Rittelmeyer writes about this as follows: 'The fact that anthroposophists did not protect him as they should have done obviously caused him far greater suffering than we knew. Opponents covered him with derision and scorn, and anthroposophists let it pass all too easily and went on enjoying his lectures. He was not concerned on account of himself as a person but on account of the effect which the disgraceful attacks would have on his work. He was fully aware that his opponents were dragging his personality into the mud in order to destroy his work. And he saw that anthroposophists did not see this; they retreated into their citadel and did not see that fire was being laid around its walls.'

This invisible fire which had been raging around the spiritual citadel of Anthroposophy for many years broke out into the open on New Year's Eve, 1922, and the First Goetheanum left the physical plane for ever in the flames. But this most tragic event in the entire history of the Anthroposophical Movement and the Anthroposophical Society hitherto demanded from Rudolf Steiner a still higher and more selfless display of tolerance and all-forgiveness. For in this case too, despite a whole series of warnings and urgent appeals on the part of Rudolf Steiner, the Anthroposophical Society was not sufficiently awake spiritually to defend the building and inwardly to protect it from its numerous powerful enemies—and hence from the catastrophe that threatened it. Rudolf Steiner referred to this state of affairs with particular clarity at an enlarged meeting of the 'Dreissiger-Kreis' on 22 January 1923, three weeks after the fire. There, having first spoken of the need to 'consolidate the Society' as soon as possible, he went on to say the following about the First Goetheanum: 'For in a certain sense what the Dornach building lacked—and which spoke forth loud and clear to the whole world—was the protective background of the Anthroposophical Society. Basically, the Anthroposophical Society declined from the moment that the building was begun.'[196]

'Ten years ... a heap of ruins'—these words of Rudolf Steiner, found in his note-book for 1923, are in their profound tragedy perhaps the clearest indication of the state of his own soul after the fire, but they do not wholly express the full tragedy of the fire for him personally. For Rudolf Steiner was, as its creator, connected with the Goetheanum, this extraordinary building which was to become an outwardly visible revelation of the being of Anthroposophia, a 'House of the Word' arising out of his etheric forces, not merely in an outward way but also karmically. After all, in order that it might come into being he had sacrificed part of his own etheric forces, which were in a mysterious way intertwined with the building's living essence. Thus the fire was at the same time a heavy blow to his own etheric body.[197]

In connection with this he wrote in a letter to Marie Steiner: 'M.d.M., I told you some while ago that since January 1923 the connection of the higher members of my being with my physical body was no longer complete: in my life in spiritual realms I had in a certain sense lost the direct connection with my physical organism. Not with the physical world.'[198] Thus as it was unable to give spiritual protection to and preserve the First Geotheanum, the Anthroposophical Society was by the same token unable to protect the etheric body of its teacher. Nevertheless, Rudolf Steiner forgave the members everything even in this trial. Moreover, he was— together with Albert Steffen—personally present at the funeral of the man who was the only person who perished in the fire and was apparently its instigator.

'During those days he was "like one great open wound"'— Friedrich Rittelmeyer cites these words of a certain anthoposophist as a means of characterizing his own impression of Rudolf Steiner in the final years of his life. And then he continues: 'And from there one may turn to the translucent calm and kindly spirit in which he wrote *The Course of my Life.*'[199]

We find not a shadow of disappointment, bitterness or reproach towards anyone in this remarkable life-story, permeated as it is with an atmosphere of the deepest good will and the most radiant gratitude towards all those people he had met in his life, towards all that he had experienced.

The Austrian writer, Max Hayek—who was sympathetic to Anthroposophy as one who had on more than one occasion attended Rudolf Steiner's public lectures in Vienna—met him in the summer of 1922. He described his impression of a meeting with him in the following words: 'He was a bearer of sorrows ... on the Earth, a martyr of the spirit, a cross-bearer.'[200]

★

The year 1923 which followed the fire was in many respects the most critical not only for the Anthroposophical Society but also for Rudolf Steiner himself. As has already been said in chapter III, at that time he more than once seriously thought and directly spoke about his intention to leave the Society, to abandon it together with a small group of his most faithful and advanced pupils. And yet, despite the ever-growing 'inner opposition' within it both to him personally and to his aims, he resolved to unite himself with it fully and irrevocably.[201] The final decision in this regard was taken by him only a few weeks before the beginning of the Christmas Conference.

Thus the bringing about of the Christmas Conference, which is associated with the complete spiritual renewal of the Anthroposophical Movement and the founding of the new Mysteries on the Earth, was possible only as a result of a *higher act of forgiveness* on the part of Rudolf Steiner, who had forgiven all the members of the Society—including his opponents—for *everything* before Him who spoke these words: 'Behold, I make all things new!' (Revelation 21:5). Only through this step was Rudolf Steiner able to bring the anthroposophical impulse to the Earth with a hitherto unprecedented power and immediacy, as the direct outpouring of new revelations from the spiritual world.

It could be said that with this deed Rudolf Steiner was fulfilling to the highest degree the demand of the Greater Guardian of the Threshold as he had described it almost 20 years before the Christmas Conference in his book *Knowledge of the Higher Worlds*:[202] 'If he [the pupil] resolves to fulfil the demands of the higher Being of Light, he will be able to contribute to the liberation of the human race. He offers up his gifts on the altar of humanity . . . But if he thus places his achievements at the disposal of humanity, he has to *renounce* all prospect of gaining anything more for himself from the scene of his future work . . . What the individual will receive in the higher regions of the supersensible world is nothing that comes to him, but entirely something that goes out from him: love for the world and for his fellows.'

It was also out of this pure 'love for the world and for his fellows' that Rudolf Steiner—in accordance with the deepest esoteric significance of these words—placed the Christmas Conference into the world.

Almost throughout the year 1923, which preceded the Christmas Conference, Rudolf Steiner was busy founding national societies everywhere in Europe in order that they might at Christmas be united in the General Anthroposophical Society, which in its individual offshoots was intended to represent humanity, to be in a certain sense a miniature reflection of it.

Thus by uniting himself with *this* Society at Christmas 1923 to the extent of his own karma, Rudolf Steiner took upon himself part of *the karma of the whole of present-day humanity*. While before the Christmas Conference such a connection on a karmic level existed only with his individual esoteric pupils or the small groups of members of the esoteric school founded by him in 1904 and which continued in existence until 1914, there was now a large international Society which had the task of openly representing the anthroposophical impulse before the whole of humanity and at the same time of representing humanity before the spiritual world and before the new Time Spirit. It was this connection with the newly founded Society on a karmic level which enabled Rudolf Steiner already during the Christmas Conference—in the evening lectures—to reveal his own karma to the anthroposophists who were present, and then—in the course of the karma lectures of 1924— also *their* karma in connection with the karma of the Anthroposophical Society and with the supersensible stream of Michael.

The inaugural *Vorstand*—in which the principal spiritual streams which in their totality form the inner configuration of the Anthroposophical Society were to find their union, reconciliation and higher synthesis—was formed by Rudolf Steiner at the Christmas Conference in the same spirit. This was the so-called 'conception of the *Vorstand*', the *Vorstand* as an esoteric reality: the uniting of *all* the karmic streams associated with the Anthroposophical Movement on the foundation of the central impulse of the Christmas Conference and in its spirit. Marie Steiner expressed this idea as follows: 'It could be an esotericism of the deepest kind to bring hitherto diverging earlier spiritual streams into harmonious equilibrium through certain of their present representatives.'[203] The spiritual task expressed in these words remains even now the central task of the *Vorstand* at the Goetheanum, and only through its ful-filment can it be enabled to work in the world also esoterically, that is, to be an 'esoteric *Vorstand*'.

Such a sacrificial taking upon himself of the karma of the *General* Anthroposophical Society and, through this, a direct participation in bearing the karma of the whole of humanity again made it apparent that Rudolf Steiner was in the deepest sense the closest colleague of Christian Rosenkreutz. And the imagination, which Rudolf Steiner gave to Ita Wegman shortly after the Christmas Conference in response to her question about his relationship to Christian Rosenkreutz, of an altar in the spiritual world beside which there stands, on the one side, Christian Rosenkreutz in a blue stole and, on the other, Rudolf Steiner in a red stole, testifies to this. In the context of the principal theme of the present work, this imagination can be understood as follows: the sacrificial altar in the centre is a symbol of Christ who, as the Lord of Karma, bears the karma of all mankind, and on His right and left are two of His greatest human assistants in this task. For just as Christian Rosenkreutz, in his service and imitation of Christ, participates in bearing the karma of humanity, taking upon himself everything which has its karmic origin in man's spiritual passivity with respect to the spiritual world (see chapter III), so with the Christmas Conference does Rudolf Steiner take upon himself the other aspect of this process, namely, all the karmic consequences of an unpurified and unenlightened striving towards the spiritual world such as is still permeated by personal ambitions and egoistic desires. This came outwardly to expression in that the consequences of such an egoistic relationship to the spiritual world on the part of many members of the Anthroposophical Society appeared in the form of those terrible occult backlashes which befell Rudolf Steiner immediately after the Christmas Conference and even while it was still in process.

Only once, and even then only in an impersonal form, did he give an indication of the tragic nature of his position. This occurred in the 'words of remembrance' which he spoke in Dornach on 3 May 1924 in memory of his pupil and colleague Edith Maryon, who had just died. Despite the length of the quotation, these words shall—because of their importance—be given here in full: 'And so you see that if you want to make a contribution in a real sense, that is, to contribute towards what the Anthroposophical Movement has become since the Christmas Conference, you must discover in these thoughts what it means to be responsible for the Anthroposophical Movement before the spiritual world ... Naturally, with those who are involved in the Anthroposophical Movement there are a large number of personal matters which come to expression. Whatever is brought about on the Earth of a personal nature is, if it is mixed up with what needs to be done on behalf of Anthroposophy, an element which—if it remains a personal affair—cannot be defended before the spiritual world. And what difficulties emerge for someone who has to be accountable to the spiritual world for some particular matter if at times he has to ally what he is responsible for with what proceeds from the personal aspirations of those who are participating in it. The effect of this is something that you ought to have at least some awareness of. It gives rise to the most terrible backlashes on the part of the spiritual world if one has to approach the spiritual world in the following sort of way.

'A certain person is working within the Anthroposophical Movement. He works within it but he introduces personal ambitions, personal intentions, personal qualities into everything he does. These personal ambitions, personal tendencies, have to be reckoned with. For the most part, people do not realize that they are personal; they mostly consider what they do to be thoroughly non-personal, because they delude themselves as to what is personal and impersonal. That has to be borne along with the rest. And this has its effect in the most dreadful backlashes from the spiritual world on the person who has to offer up to the spiritual world these things which have their source in the personal element.'[204]

These 'most terrible ... most dreadful backlashes' which after the Christmas Conference exerted their influence upon the very physical sheath of Rudolf Steiner—for karmic forces always work through to the physical body—served as the deeper, occult reason for his premature death. However, Rudolf Steiner—like Christian Rosenkreutz—in his service and imitation of the Christ Being never for one moment sought to defend himself from these inner blows but bore them with the greatest tolerance to the end, as before forgiving all those who—mostly without their being aware of it— deprived him of the possibility of remaining on Earth and com- pleting what he had begun after the Christmas Conference.

And if the two closest colleagues of Rudolf Steiner, Marie Steiner and Ita Wegman, tell us that, according to his own testimony, the principal cause of his premature death was that he had taken upon himself the heavy karma of the Anthroposophical Society,[205] then this—perhaps the deepest mystery of Rudolf Steiner's life and at the same time of the Anthroposophical Movement and the Anthro- posophical Society—is likewise connected in a very direct way with the mystery of forgiveness. This thought can also be expressed in a more religious form, in the language of the fundamental Christian prayer, as Friedrich Rittelmeyer has done: 'Rudolf Steiner died at the hand of human "sins" ... His freely given help led him to death.'[206] Here one could also say 'his forgiving help', this being a consequence of his having again and again forgiven. This is what Marie Steiner had in mind when she wrote in her 'Appeal for Reconciliation' about the 'sacrifice' of Rudolf Steiner and about his 'death', 'for which we are all surely guilty both as individuals and as a Society.'[207]

The same thought and the same words—though raised to a cosmic dimension—could also be said of Christ, 'who took upon Himself the sins of the world' (John 1:29) and who for the further help of humanity remained with it until His death on the Cross and thereafter in the spirit for all ages to come.

★

Everything that has been said here about Rudolf Steiner also has a direct relationship to his pupils—not only to those who were his contemporaries but likewise to all who come after. For in that constant forgiving which he accomplished throughout his life, we have not only a high example but also a kind of spiritual 'covenant'. If we really want to become spiritually close to him, it is not enough merely to know about his achievements or to have a general wish to serve his cause. Rather it is necessary to make every possible effort to follow *his* path, however difficult it may be, truly to follow him in a small way just as he, on a much larger scale, followed the highest Archetype: the path of Christ Himself.

This means a conscious endeavour to unite one's own destiny, even one's karma (in a deeper sense it cannot be otherwise),[208] with the General Anthroposophical Society to which Rudolf Steiner quite literally sacrificed *everything*. Neither should we turn away from or ignore all its former difficulties (or those that continue to exist now), unresolved problems and patently evident inadequacies nor forget or allow ourselves to be ignorant about its so very tragic history, but rather, as we find ourselves within it—by beholding it from the standpoint of the higher, universally human tasks placed before the Society by Rudolf Steiner in the present age of Michael—try to fulfil that process of 'moral breathing' which was spoken of earlier: receiving or 'inhaling' into ourselves its tragic past and difficult present, however agonizing and arduous this may be, and 'exhaling' those new spiritual forces, that moral substance—whose presence in the Society is the principal sign of our inner faithfulness to Rudolf Steiner and the guarantee of our relationship with him.

The most significant example of such 'moral breathing' in the history of the Anthroposophical Movement is to be found in the process whereby the Foundation Stone Meditation came into being, a process which is in a remarkable way associated with that spiritual metamorphosis through which the being of the Goetheanum passed when, borne up by fire, it rose into the heights of the etheric cosmos. All the evil of this demonic, destructive deed was taken up by Rudolf Steiner into his etheric body, inwardly transformed by his spirit and then returned to the world as a higher good—returned not only through the uninterrupted and still more intense spiritual work in the course of the year that followed but, above all, in the formulating of the Foundation Stone Meditation at the Christmas Conference as a new cosmic revelation (clothed in human words) of that Spirit who was manifested on the Earth in the visible forms of the First Goetheanum and then, with the flames of the fire, passed over into the spiritual world.

Rudolf Steiner himself spoke about the living 'Spirit of the

Goetheanum', and about the fact that much of what was said at the Christmas Conference was spoken 'in contemplation of' this Spirit, in his reply to the words of gratitude addressed to him by Louis Werbeck on behalf of all those present at the conclusion of the Conference on 1 January 1924.[209]

This 'good Spirit of the Goetheanum' was to become ever more a kind of 'group soul' of the General Anthroposophical Society. For just as in the physically visible Goetheanum—the visible expression of the being of Anthroposophia—individuals who had hitherto belonged to different karmic streams were to find a harmonious unity through gradually gaining a knowledge of their common karma,[210] so after its transformation does the 'Spirit of the Goetheanum' springing from the cosmos wish to be the inspiring Spirit of the new, and far more conscious, uniting of these streams, which rests upon the foundation of a full knowledge of the heavenly karma of the Anthroposophical Society in its relationship with the cosmic stream of Michael.

In this sense, 'intercourse' with the 'Spirit of the Goetheanum' can become a possibility for every anthroposophist if—in addition to his firm endeavour to remain true to the fundamental impulse of Anthroposophy as it was manifested at the Christmas Conference and in what followed it—he at the same time directs his inner efforts towards developing those initial qualities of the Manichaean path, the spiritual-scientific consideration of which has been the purpose of this book.

★

It has already been observed (chapter VI, 4) that any true act of forgiveness is so difficult for modern man because its fulfilment is unavoidably connected with passing through a condition of total powerlessness before destiny, of total defencelessness before the evil that is to be forgiven. Herein lies what is perhaps the principal difficulty in responding to evil *not* with violence but with forgiveness and gentleness.

On the other hand, it is precisely this that is the very essence of the Mystery of Golgotha, when from complete outer powerlessness and defencelessness—culminating with the crucifixion of the God who had become man alongside two robbers—is born a new impulse, the impulse of the *Resurrection* which transforms the whole of earthly existence.

We find a reflection of this profound mystery in the mystery of the Christmas Conference, for the bringing about of which Rudolf Steiner had to accomplish something whose consequences were unknown even to himself. For by taking upon himself the chairmanship of the newly founded Anthroposophical Society, and hence also the responsibility for its earthly affairs, he was in fact risking his *entire spiritual mission* and was acting in full awareness that there was a real possibility that the spiritual world—or to be more precise the spiritual beings ruling over anthroposophical wisdom—might not accept his deed and might close off from him the sources of the revelations which had hitherto unfailingly nourished the Anthroposophical Movement. This moment was indeed the most difficult and dramatic in Rudolf Steiner's destiny as a teacher of mankind, and made the Christmas Conference an event that was for him like the Mystery of Golgotha,[211] like passing in the deepest humility and submissiveness through a complete inner powerlessness and defencelessness before the awaited answer of world karma, before the decision of the spiritual world. Indeed, by uniting himself with the earthly organization of the Society, Rudolf Steiner was entering the sphere of activity of the most concentrated death-forces in earthly evolution, whence no one can escape through his own forces unless he be led forth by the only divine Being who has overcome death.

Already considerably earlier, in the lecture of 16 October 1918, Rudolf Steiner referred to two decisive inner events which had led to a spiritual experience of the Mystery of Golgotha in his own destiny. He termed them 'powerlessness' and 'resurrection from powerlessness': 'This twofold experience really leads us towards the Mystery of Golgotha.'[212]

And when, from the abyss of powerlessness, there finally came an answer from the spiritual world bearing resurrection forces, an answer in the form of the new, still mightier and more all-embracing revelations to which Rudolf Steiner referred again and again in his karma lectures, only his own words from the same lecture can express what actually took place in his soul: 'But when we can experience powerlessness and the recovery from it, we find that we are blessed with a true relationship with Christ Jesus . . . And anyone who is able to speak of the two experiences of powerlessness and the resurrection from it is speaking of the true Christ experience. For he has found his way to the Mystery of Golgotha along a supersensible path, he has discovered for himself the powers which stir certain supersensible faculties into activity and lead him to the Mystery of Golgotha.'

This means that Christ was that higher power through whom, having followed Him, Rudolf Steiner consciously entered that realm of powerlessness and death whence—in answer to the sacrifice that he made, the depth of which we can only guess— *Christ Himself* led him forth as a pupil of His who had sacrificed *everything* on his path of initiation.

★

To conclude, mention should be made of a further aspect of Rudolf Steiner's mission among mankind, one which relates to the three higher stages of that sevenfold Manichean Path which was described in chapter V.

As has already been explained by the present author in the book *Rudolf Steiner and the Founding of the New Mysteries*, the central experience in Rudolf Steiner's inner development was his encounter with the Christ Being in the sphere of Intuition, as the Cosmic Archetype of every human ego. This fundamental experience in Rudolf Steiner's inner life took place around the year 1899. He refers to this at the end of the twenty-sixth chapter of his autobiography, *The Course of My Life*, and gives a spiritual-scientific description of it in the chapter entitled 'Knowledge of Higher Worlds' in *Occult Science—An Outline*.[213]

From an occult point of view, this event signified that from that time forth Christ was able to be present within and work through Rudolf Steiner's higher ego. And this relationship with Christ gave him the inner right to appear at the beginning of the twentieth century as the spiritual teacher and representative of the central stream of Christian esotericism. In the latter sense, the stage which he had attained of a conscious experience of Christ corresponded to the highest fulfilment of the words of Paul the Apostle, 'Not I, but Christ in me'. Thenceforth, by bearing the *Spiritual Sun* at the very centre of his being, in his ego, Rudolf Steiner was gradually able to fill his sheaths with its light, life and love. An outer reflection of this process could be discerned in that it was possible for him to participate in the redemption of the opposing forces.

The most immediate task that was placed before Rudolf Steiner in this direction was determined through the fact of his joining the Theosophical Society in the year 1902. For since H.P. Blavatsky had written her *Secret Doctrine*, the principal occult characteristic of this society had been the inner conviction on the part of its leading circles of the spiritual superiority of Lucifer over Yahveh and, hence, over Christ who had in ancient times worked *through* Yahveh. This was the reason for the markedly anti-Christian bias of the Theosophical Society, which was fully and exclusively orientated towards the Tibeto-Indian occultism of the East, this being the last remnant of the ancient luciferic wisdom of mankind.[214] Thus 'Blavatsky was led by certain beings who had an interest in enticing her to place Lucifer in Christ's stead ...'[215] 'Hence the assertion in the *Secret Doctrine* that one should not attach oneself to Yahveh ... [and that] the true benefactor of mankind is Lucifer. The whole of the *Secret Doctrine* is constructed in such a way that this shines through it, and it is also made fully explicit. Thus H.P. Blavatsky had to be prepared as a hater of Christ-Yahveh for occult reasons.'[216] From the very beginning, Rudolf Steiner opposed this anti-Christian tendency—behind which quite specific, national group-interests of certain circles of Tibeto-Indian occultists were concealed[217]—through the wisdom of Rosicrucian Christianity, a wisdom which pursued only universally human aims and has its source not in the Lucifer who fights against Christ but in the Lucifer who is transformed by Christ and serves Him.[218]

In an esoteric sense this was possible because, through setting the light of the Sun of Christ over and against Lucifer in his astral body, Rudolf Steiner was able to participate directly in the redemption of this being. For this reason, Lucifer is spoken of far more frequently and at greater length in the earlier lectures (until approximately 1909) than Ahriman.

★

The next stage was represented by the first steps on the path towards the redemption of Ahriman. However, a beginning towards his redemption can be made not by individual spiritually striving human beings but through the social activity which they have in common. Here we have the occult source of those practical anthroposophical initiatives at whose foundation there lie those activities which people carry out *together*: the movement for the threefolding of the social organism, the arising of the Waldorf schools, the Movement for Religious Renewal (the Christian Community), and above all the founding at the beginning of 1913 of the independent Anthroposophical Society and in the autumn of the same year the laying of the Foundation Stone of the First Goetheanum in Dornach as its visible centre.

In all these diverse undertakings there are the seeds of that shared human endeavour which has the power to transform and spiritualize modern culture and which to the extent of its diffusion amongst mankind will be able to offer a means of help—on the basis of the anthroposophical conception of the world—whereby the physical incarnation of Ahriman on the Earth,[219] which is by no means very far away, might be directed towards the good of further evolution and thus further the latter's redemption in the future.

Rudolf Steiner was himself in the position to found all the movements enumerated above only through the fact that he was able to let the forces of the Christ Sun—which had entered into his ego at the turn of the century—flow into his etheric body, where they became *life*. This Christ-life he then set over and against Ahriman in all areas of human creativity—which could therefore have its foundation in an activity of the etheric body permeated by the forces of Christ. This work was unfolded with particular intensity after the end of the First World War and continued on until the last months of Rudolf Steiner's earthly life. Among these initiatives were: anthroposophical medicine, Biodynamic agriculture, the beginning of the renewal of the sciences in the spirit of Goetheanism, and Waldorf education.

At this time, the theme of Lucifer and his redemption increasingly withdraws into the background, while into the foreground there steps the need for as comprehensive a knowledge as possible of the being, aims and characteristic behaviour of Ahriman and of the spirits that serve him. Beginning with the lectures entitled *The Karma of Untruthfulness*, this theme is developed further and reaches its full power in the cycle *The Fall of the Spirits of Darkness*, which was given in Dornach in the autumn of 1917. In these lectures, the description of the Time Spirit, Michael, in his battle with the ahrimanic spirits is placed at the very centre.

In a certain sense one can say that the gradual transition from one theme to the other is brought about in such a way that the first—the theme of the 'knowledge of Lucifer'—reaches a certain culmination in the lecture-cycle *Man in the Light of Occultism, Theosophy and Philosophy*, which was given in the summer of 1912, while the new theme—that of the 'knowledge of Ahriman'—emerges in connection with the *deed* of the laying of the Foundation Stone of the First Goetheanum in September 1913. Again, the most active development of the first of these comes about principally in the early period of Rudolf Steiner's spiritual-scientific activity,[220] while the development of the second takes place in a later period. Between these two 'poles' stretched the middle epoch, the period of the most intense development of anthroposophical art—where both themes maintained an inner equilibrium. At approximately the mid-point of this middle period came Rudolf Steiner's lectures on the Fifth Gospel.

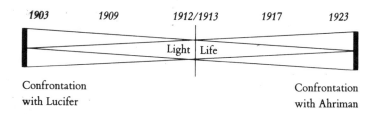

1903	First article in the magazine *Lucifer* (later called *Lucifer-Gnosis*)
1909	Lecture-cycle *The East in the Light of the West. The Children of Lucifer and the Brothers of Christ*
1912/1913	Lecture-cycle *Man in the Light of Occultism, Theosophy and Philosophy* Founding of the Anthroposophical Society Laying of the Foundation Stone of the First Goetheanum
1917	Lecture-cycle *The Fall of the Spirits of Darkness*
1923	Lectures on the festival of Michaelmas

Among the artistic achievements of this middle period can be included all the Mystery Plays, the creation of Eurythmy, and of course all those many artistic initiatives in the most diverse realms which came to expression in the construction of the First Goetheanum.

In the context of our theme, the following words spoken by Rudolf Steiner in characterization of the building are of particular importance: 'Just consider the forms of our building: everywhere the straight line is led over into the curve, balance is sought; everywhere the attempt is made to dissolve what is fixed into a fluid element, everywhere rest is created out of movement, but a rest which is again translated into movement. That is what is truly spiritual in our building. We must, as people of the future, endeavour to create in both art and life something whereby we may know: down there is Ahriman who wants to make everything become rigid, up there is Lucifer who wants to waft everything away ... And so our building has become a state of equilibrium in the universe which has been wrested and removed from the realm of Ahriman and the realm of Lucifer.'[221] This state of equilibrium attained its highest manifestation in the sculptural Group which depicts in *artistic form* the Representative of Man, Christ, as the Archetype of the group ego of mankind, and at the same time of the higher ego of each individual human being, between Lucifer and

Ahriman: 'Everything culminates in the central figure of our Group, in this Representative of Man in whom all that pertains to Lucifer and Ahriman shall be obliterated.'

At this point it is appropriate to introduce the striking story, transmitted by Heinz Müller, about the way that Rudolf Steiner created the sculptural Group. Müller reports that 'he needed both Lucifer and Ahriman to sit for him as a model. In the case of Ahriman this was managed only through the use of a considerable degree of coercion, while Lucifer acquiesced relatively easily with this situation.'[222] Both spirits had to serve as models for as long as it took him to finish his work. Only then had he, Rudolf Steiner, brought the sitting to an end—because, in his own words: 'Present-day humanity would have to try to form clear pictures of the opposing forces and thereby rob them of their power.' It was roughly at this time that Rudolf Steiner said in one of his lectures in Dornach: 'What is the most profound characteristic of our epoch and of the evolution of the consciousness soul? The profoundest characteristic of this epoch is that man must become acquainted in the most thorough and most intense way with all those forces that oppose the harmonizing of humanity as a whole. For this reason a conscious knowledge of those ahrimanic and luciferic powers working against man must gradually spread in our time.'[223]

In order that we may understand this seemingly almost incredible story of Heinz Müller from an occult point of view, it is necessary to take into account that only the *light* of the Christ Sun working in the astral body of the initiate could keep Lucifer in his power, just as only the *life* of the Christ Sun working in his etheric body could keep Ahriman in his power.

In other words, the creation of the sculptural Group was the direct consequence of the attainment by Rudolf Steiner, the Christian initiate of modern times, of the higher stages of the Manichaean path described in the present work, a path which has as its focus—as is the case also with the modern Rosicrucian path—the conscious experience of Christ in one's ego and the resultant possibility of a direct encounter with Him in the spiritual world. And so, Rudolf Steiner was (according to his own testimony) able—both in the sculptural Group and in the central motif of the paintings of the small cupola of the Goetheanum—to portray Christ as He is revealed *in our time* to the initiate in the etheric world nearest to the Earth. Heinz Müller recalls this as follows: 'Then Rudolf Steiner went on to speak about the similarity between his study and the countenance of Christ. If one were to meet Him in the spiritual world, one's first impression would be that it changes to a surprisingly marked degree with every thought, feeling and will impulse ... Now, as His Being is abiding in the ethereal heights free from the body of Jesus of Nazareth, this constant changing of His countenance increases even more. In spite of this, however—Rudolf Steiner assured us—the forms and also the colours of the Representative of Man were fashioned in such a way that if one were to encounter Him [in the etheric world] one would recognize Him immediately. Thus in this case too one could quite definitely speak of a kind of verisimilitude.'

Similarly, Rudolf Steiner said to the Swiss anthroposophist Willi Aeppli (who was visiting him in his studio in Dornach), in response to a question that stirred within him but was not actually verbalized, pointing to the figure of Christ from the sculptural Group: 'Yes, that is how I saw Him.'[224] And in the lecture of 29 June 1921, which is devoted to a detailed description of the sculptural and painted forms of the First Goetheanum, he explained the source of the figure of Christ in the small cupola as follows: 'One can imagine it [the Representative of Man] to be the Christ. I have formed it wholly out of my visionary perception as a figure of Christ ... Naturally, I have no need that anyone believes this, but it is Christ as He stood before my Spirit vision ... Christ stands there as the embodiment of love.'[225]

★

In general, Rudolf Steiner speaks remarkably little about the last category of opposing powers, the so-called Asuras. Apart from some fleeting references to them in his earlier lectures,[226] detailed information about them is to be found only in the above-quoted lecture of 22 March 1909.[227] The next—again very brief—reference to them is contained in the lecture of 15 December 1919 in

Dornach,[228] after which, right until the end of his earthly activity, Rudolf Steiner never speaks of them again—the reason being that he was concentrating his efforts to an ever-increasing degree upon gaining knowledge of and withstanding the forces of Ahriman in view of the latter's impending incarnation amongst mankind.

As regards the Asuric spirits, Rudolf Steiner—in the last of the lectures referred to—characterizes them as beings who bear 'cultural sickness, cultural death'[229] to earthly civilization, an influence which humanity will be able to withstand only to the extent that the principal aims of the new Mysteries will be attained on the Earth.

'The world must in our time find the way to receive once more the principle of initiation as such among the principles of civilization.'[230] In these words the only means of withstanding the Asuric temptation is given to the whole of mankind and especially to anthroposophists, a countervailing force which is at the same time also a path which leads to their redemption—which will begin only when the new Mysteries and the 'principle of initiation associated with them has spread over the entire Earth and has taken over the leadership of earthly civilization. These will be Mysteries where the Christ Sun will shine forth not only as a *light* bestowing higher knowledge upon human being's astral bodies, not only as a new *life in imaginations*, which will then arise in people's etheric bodies and thence flow forth into social life, forming and transforming it, but they will be Mysteries which will be manifested as penetrating to the physical body and permeating it with the Resurrection forces of the *love* of Christ, which is alone capable of overcoming 'sickness and death' within man and, hence, in earthly culture as a whole.

The foundation of these new Christian Mysteries was laid by Rudolf Steiner at the Christmas Conference of 1923/24. Since that time, as a seed for their gradual evolution among mankind, the possibility has been given to the hearts and souls of all true anthroposophists of the past, present and future of laying within themselves the Foundation Stone that was formed by Rudolf Steiner on 25 December 1923 in the etheric world nearest to the Earth out of the forces of the Holy Trinity—of the Spirit, the Son and the Father—working in our cosmos: 'Out of these three forces:

out of the Spirit of the heights, out of the force of Christ in the circumference, out of the working of the Father, the creative activity of the Father that streams out of the depths, let us at this moment give form in our souls to the dodecahedral Foundation Stone which we lower into the soil of our souls so that it may remain there as a powerful sign in the strong foundations of our soul existence and so that in the future working of the Anthroposophical Society we may stand on this firm Foundation Stone.'[231]

The Foundation Stone, which since then has served as the foundation of the soul-life of every true anthroposophist, was formed from the forces of the Spirit which come from the heights and lead to the overcoming of the power of Lucifer; from the forces of Christ which work in the surroundings of the Earth and lead to the overcoming of the power of Ahriman amongst mankind; and from the forces of the Father which proceed from the depths and lead to the overcoming of the power of the Asuras in earthly evolution.[232] Man can, however, lay this 'dodecahedral Stone of love', this 'dodecahedral imagination of love', into his own heart, into his own soul—and thereby enter upon the path of the new Mysteries—only if he aspires with his whole being towards the

Light Divine,
Christ-Sun

that shines forth at the Turning Point of Time, from the sources of which the world light, the world life-bestowing imaginations[233] and the world love—the cosmic expression of the world Trinity—can flow forth into man's being.[234]

And just as in the universe like always strives towards like, so can this world Trinity be received on Earth only by the human threefoldness that is akin to it: by human light, by the human capacity for life in imaginations and by human love. For if we bring to Christ the spiritual *light* of higher knowledge which arises from a selfless experiencing of spiritual-scientific thoughts, if we bring to Him our faculty of living in *imaginations* which is won through meditative work and from thence extends its influence upon our social surroundings, and, finally, if we bring to Him our sacrificial *love*, spiritualized and purified from all egoism, our human light will be strengthened by His World Light, our human imaginations will be strengthened by His World Imaginations, and our spiritualized human love will be strengthened by His World Love. Then there will arise on the Earth 'a true community of human beings for Anthroposophia' to which neither Lucifer (who appropriates light only for himself), nor Ahriman (who blots out imaginations and freezes everything that lives), nor the Asuras (who bring death to all love) will gain access.

'Then shall the Foundation Stone shine forth before the eyes of our soul, that Foundation Stone which has received its substance from universal love and human love; its picture image, its form, from universal imagination and human imagination; and its brilliant radiance from universal thoughts and human thoughts—its brilliant radiance which whenever we recollect this moment can shine towards us with warm light, with light that spurs on our deeds, our thinking, our feeling and our will.' 'That good may become' what we found in the world through our deeds that proceed from a thinking which is permeated with *tolerance*, from a feeling which is able to *forgive*, and from a will which strives to participate in the creation of a new *karmic community* of human beings on Earth. Then the 'Spirit that rules in the shining light of thoughts around the dodecahedral Stone of Love' as the Spirit of the new Michael Mysteries, who is alone capable of leading mankind into the future in the sense of the intentions of Michael-Christ, will be able to stream forth into the whole of earthly evolution, 'where it shall give of its light and of its warmth for the progress of human souls, for the progress of the universe.'

★

Thus we may find in the Christmas Conference an archetype and at the same time the quintessence of that path which we have endeavoured to delineate in the present work. It follows from this that an approach to its spiritual essence is not to be arrived at through abstract thoughts as one would in the case of a past event but through *real inner activity*, through the gradual inner transforming of the whole of one's humanity in the course of developing the qualities of tolerance, forgiveness and the capacity of bearing the karma of others. For the Christmas Conference reveals its spiritual essence only to one who strives to approach it with the help of those same spiritual impulses out of which it was placed 66 years ago into 'the stream of earthly being' by its inspirer and creator—Rudolf Steiner.

Postscript

The need for the postscript that follows has arisen as a result of questions put to the author at his lectures on the occult significance of forgiveness, which were given in various towns of Europe while the present book was being written.

Above all else it is necessary to emphasize with absolute clarity that forgiveness in a Manichaean sense does not by any means signify simply non-resistance to evil. On the contrary, if one is to exclude the use of any form of outer or inner violence towards another person, any mistake or error—and especially any evil or falsehood—on his part must be counteracted by a strong will for what is good and true directed (to the extent of one's forces and possibilities) towards the rectification of what has been done. In other words, fairly often in life one finds oneself in situations where forgiveness needs to remain a purely *inner act*, while outwardly a courageous and fearless response to evil and falsehood is required.

It is quite another situation where the forgiveness of one's own mistakes and inadequacies is concerned. Rudolf Steiner writes about this in *Knowledge of the Higher Worlds: How is it Achieved?*: 'Directly you try to excuse to yourself any one of your weaknesses, you have laid a stone in the path that is to lead you upwards.'[235] This means that for the spiritual world only a rectification of errors and shortcomings that is carried out on the basis of true self-knowledge—or, at any rate, an endeavour to achieve this—has any significance.

The same can be said of 'excuses'. Where they are not accompanied by a will that is directed towards actually rectifying what has been done, they have no significance for the spiritual world. If we also take into account that the tendency to make excuses is an outer expression of that soul process which is usually called 'remorse', we may better understand the following remark of Rudolf Steiner: 'Remorse has no value. One must make good; that shortens kamaloka.'[236]

Of course, if 'remorse' is understood as part of real self-knowledge it has considerable significance for the individual concerned, for all mistakes and errors must first be understood objectively before one can begin to put them right. However, 'remorse' which derives from self-flagellation and self-torture and, as it were, covers the soul's horizon with dark, suffocating clouds, thus ultimately leading to inner wretchedness and even to despair, not only harms the human soul but, as we have seen, has no positive significance for the spiritual world.

All in all one can say: when a person who has done something bad is sincerely sorry, he enters upon the path of balancing out the negative karma of the past (Moon karma), the karma which he has himself caused through his deed. Such a deed in an occult sense destroys the moral structure of the world, diminishes the perfection of the spiritual cosmos. So a person who endeavours to make good all the consequences of his wrongful deed is able to restore to the spiritual cosmos that same degree of perfection which it had before.

Where, on the other hand, an individual is able wholly and without reservation to forgive the person who has caused him harm, there arises now, positive karma, or *Sun* karma. With remorse there begins a balancing out of the past, with forgiveness the creation of the future. In the latter case it is not merely a question of restoring the lost level of perfection of the spiritual cosmos but of raising it to a new stage which it did not have *before* the act of forgiveness. As a result of this the spiritual cosmos together with all the Hierarchies comes a step closer to that perfection which culminates in likeness to its Creator.

However, while forgiving oneself merely holds one back in one's inner development, this does not mean that the achievement of forgiveness, or—expressed in more traditional language—the 'remission of sins', is impossible in a purely spiritual sense as an inner mystery of the soul. The spiritual process which in such a case can take place in the soul is one of the most important experiences of modern man. What is meant by this is the following.

In the present epoch of the consciousness soul, the principal goal of western humanity is the attainment by an ever greater number of people of a wholly individual and fully conscious relationship to the Christ Being. As has been shown in the present book, one of the means of attaining this goal is 'the way to the Christ through thinking', which leads through the stages of tolerance, forgiveness and taking upon oneself the karma of another person. This path is also associated with the new, Manichaean experience of good and evil in their relationship to the repetition of the Mystery of Golgotha in the supersensible world nearest to the Earth, and to the new appearance of Christ in the etheric form in which He will, from our time onwards, gradually reveal Himself to humanity. Because of this, and in full harmony with the fundamental character of the present epoch of freedom, the extent of man's participation in the process of the redeeming (spiritualizing) of himself and the world must grow significantly, and this is possible only through the attainment of a personal and conscious relationship to the Christ Being.

In this process, a decisive part will be played by 'Christ-filled spiritual science' or Anthroposophy, which in its esoteric nature is that language in which humanity in our time can converse directly with the Etheric Christ (see chapter II), which means to enter into an inner, intimately personal relationship with Him such as can enable one in meditation to receive from Him true 'forgiveness of sins'. Rudolf Steiner refers to this possibility as follows: 'Those who assimilate Christ-filled spiritual science in the right spirit and not merely in an external sense can most assuredly become their own father confessors. Most assuredly through spiritual science they will learn to know Christ so intimately, and feel themselves so closely connected with Him, that they can be directly conscious of His spiritual presence. And when they have solemnly sworn allegiance to Him as the cosmic Principle, they will be able to direct their confession to Him in spirit, and in their silent meditation ask from Him forgiveness of sins ... In earthly life this may all be an ideal, but the anthroposophist may at least look up to such an ideal.'[237]

It will, however, be possible to approach this ideal only if the two principal conditions that are necessary for a true act of forgiveness are fulfilled: self-overcoming, that is, overcoming all the egoistic inclinations of the lower ego, and surrendering oneself in love to the world, a readiness for sacrificial service. These two soul qualities also play a truly central part in modern spirit-pupilship. Thus at a higher stage of inner development they prepare the pupil for the meeting respectively with the Lesser and the Greater Guardian of the Threshold. For the first of these Guardians continually demands for his purification the overcoming—through true self-knowledge—of all the influences of the lower ego which draw one down, while the second personifies with His whole Being that service to the world which is permeated with sacrificial love.[238]

Taken together, these two qualities form the necessary pre-requisite for an inner 'remission of sins' by Christ in the sense of the above words of Rudolf Steiner. For only he who possesses these qualities, which is to say is *capable* of true forgiveness, can also hope for forgiveness on the part of Christ—as is indicated with full clarity in the fifth petition of the Lord's Prayer: 'And forgive us our debts, as we also have forgiven our debtors.'

★

The second question which again and again arises in connection with the theme of forgiveness is as follows: does the fact of the forgiveness of the person who has done a wrong deed have any significance if he *outwardly* has no knowledge of this (maybe because he has moved elsewhere or because of physical death)? In the first place, it should be observed that forgiveness has in any event a decisive significance for the meeting of *both* human beings in the spiritual world after their death—not only in the sense that every act of forgiveness that is accomplished alleviates and shortens the time that the person who has forgiven spends in kamaloka, but particularly because the new relationship with Christ that has arisen through the act of forgiveness enables the person who has forgiven to enter after death into a completely different relationship to the person who has been forgiven than would otherwise have been the case (see chapter VI, 4). On the other hand, non-forgiveness makes the relationship of a dead person with a living person, upon whom he has inflicted some wrong while still on Earth, considerably more difficult. As he beholds his wrongful action in kamaloka in all its cosmic significance, the dead person naturally directs his gaze down to that person before whom he is guilty. But if the latter has not forgiven him, the dead person is unable to gain access to his soul in his yearning to put right what he has done. This significantly aggravates his sufferings in kamaloka and also burdens the karma of both, thus strengthening the power of iron necessity in the spiritual world.

As regards the next earthly life, an act of true forgiveness that is accompanied by a resolve to return to the world as much goodness and love as was taken from it by the wrongful action can after death lead the soul to the decision to meet the person, who has inflicted suffering upon it, again on Earth, though now not in order to 'receive' back from him the good that is karmically due to it but in order to *help* the person, who has wronged it, again to attain that degree of inner perfection which he forfeited as a result of perpetrating this deed. Thus a person's meeting with an individual or a group of human beings whom he has forgiven in the next earthly life can signify not only the payment of a previous debt—as, to give a classical example, happened in the case of Pestalozzi[239]—but can also be the beginning of an entirely new karma, freely undertaken in the sense of the higher intentions of Christ as the Lord of Karma. This is also a kind of 'moral breathing' (see chapter VI), though extending its influence not through one but through two or several successive earthly lives.

Of course, a person who has inflicted an injury on another is not freed through forgiveness from the karmic necessity of manifesting to him in the next life (or lives) as much goodness and love as he had formerly manifested of evil. The law of karma continues to work here with an iron necessity. But through forgiveness—which is always associated from a spritual point of view with a voluntary renunciation of a future 'requital'—the ways in which karma is balanced out can become altogether different. For the goodness and love which a person, who in a particular earthly life has perpetrated an evil deed, would—in the event of non-forgiveness—necessarily have to return to the other person in the next life can—through forgiveness—be used in the spiritual cosmos in a completely different way, as goodness and love that have been freely sacrificed to the world and to its further evolution in the spirit of the aims and intentions of Christ as the Lord of Karma. 'To ensure that in future our karmic account may be balanced—that is, when in the future we have found our way to Christ, that it will be accepted into the cosmic order in such a way that the process of compensating for our karma may serve the greatest possible good of mankind for the rest of human evolution—this will be the concern of Him who from our time onwards will be the Lord of Karma, this will be the concern of Christ,' said Rudolf Steiner in this connection.[240]

Finally, there are those cases where an individual—at any rate for a certain portion of his life's path—has neither enemies nor people with respect to whom he has something to forgive. 'I have nothing to forgive anyone for,' such people can be heard saying. Of course, such an observation can simply be the result of insufficient self-knowledge. But perhaps it is the case—especially if such a situation in life is combined with a complete fulfilment of one's destiny—that a situation of this kind really is the result of a particularly favourable karma, for example, the result of numerous acts of forgiveness in past lives. It is true that such periods in life are for the most part only temporary, and difficulties and problems sooner or later recur anyway. However, such a karmically 'happy period' can and must be used for the development of a heightened sense of gratitude for everything that happens to and around a person, a feeling which changes into what Rudolf Steiner characterizes as 'all-embracing love' towards the world.[241] Such a love leads a person in the next earthly life (and in certain cases already in this one) to life situations where the need for 'moral breathing' is particularly great. Moreover, he will be able to help other people far more effectively, and especially those who in their present earthly life are least capable of forgiveness. All this will, however, come about not through the necessity of his personal karma but 'at the behest of' higher powers.

Such a consciously developed sense of gratitude towards one's destiny and everything that happens to one becomes an especially powerful and dynamic spiritual force in the case of a particularly difficult karma or as a result of enduring especially great sufferings and evil. For it is extremely challenging to maintain this feeling in difficult life circumstances. The only thing that can help here is real progress on the path of spirit-pupilship, such as is associated with the development of the capacity to transform the wrong that has been inflicted on one into inner wisdom, into a constant longing to find in the sufferings, injustices or blows of fate which one has experienced a *higher spiritual meaning*. What has traditionally been called 'God's providence' can—for an individual who follows the path of modern spirit-pupilship and has through Anthroposophy familiarized himself with the spiritual essence of the laws of karma and reincarnation—become a consciously experienced Manichaean initiation, which leads to an experience of the presence and working of the Etheric Christ as the Lord of Karma, both in his own destiny and in the spiritual destiny of all mankind.

Of course, the stronger the karmic connection between people and groups of people, the harder forgiveness turns out to be. On the other hand, the more inner forces are necessary for forgiveness the more significant the fruits of forgiveness will be for the person's life after death and for all his subsequent earthly lives. For the situation which caused the problem of forgiveness to arise with the power that was manifest in the case of Simon Wiesenthal always springs from the deepest karmic foundations; in its spiritual essence it is none other than an inner question about the Christ, called forth by an unconscious approach to His spiritual sphere.

In this sense one can say: the acuteness of the problem of forgiveness in our time is both a reflection of the need for a new, conscious relationship to Christ, and for the revelation of the higher spiritual meaning and world mission of *forgiveness* that is associated with it—a revelation which is now possible through modern spiritual science or Anthroposophy.

Appendix 1

The text of an 'Appeal for Reconciliation' by Marie Steiner*

Dornach, 12 December 1942

To the members of the Anthroposophical Society in Switzerland

One hears much about the problems which concern the members of our Society. And how should this be otherwise? To be sure, they appear before one's eyes from every side, some of an external and some of an internal nature; to a certain extent they are even mutually dependent on one another. In so far as they are of an inward nature and, hence, bear a soul and individual aspect, they ultimately derive from the judgement of the individual. Their outward manifestation is strongly related to the brutally destructive harshness of contemporary events. For everything of a productive nature, all initiatives of any substance are gradually overwhelmed and suppressed by the powers of the day; one stands before the merciless destruction of what has already been created and fulfilled.

In this inner storm and outer struggle the spirit hears what scarce it comprehends: the man who overcomes himself finds freedom from the power that binds all living creatures.

What in the last few centuries could be achieved in the consciousness of the individual must now gradually be mastered by

* Taken from *Marie Steiner: Briefe und Dokumente vornehmlich aus ihrem letzten Lebensjahr* (Correspondence and Documents stemming mainly from the last year of her life), Dornach 1981.

groups, by communities. However, no task is more difficult, for a community is a fluctuating mass; it constantly changes not merely its outward aspect but also its inner countenance. Hardly has a stratum of humanity attained through many struggles and experiences a more mature stage of consciousness, then the next generation—or those who were previously standing somewhat apart—thrusts itself forward as its successors who now have to begin anew with gathering experiences and who, as a result, drive the stage of maturity that has been reached back to an earlier, less mature stage. When old problems confront this younger generation, judgements are made and gladly so; they are most ready to say what they think—but for the most part they lack the necessary foundation for making judgements. In complicated cases they are altogether unable to manage this. All manner of rumours are bandied about, and this means that not only do forms become protean in their variety but that substance itself is falsified, facts are often even changed into their opposite. As conflicts have been built up over years and decades, their real value is lost through sympathies and antipathies and through being subjected to people's desires. Anyone who has not participated knowingly in everything from the start will soon be entangled in an impenetrable web and will see spectres, not realities. He gropes in the dark, the truth evades him.

Now every generation is cleverer than the one before—for it takes on the intellectual progress which has been made by those who have gone before and leads it further. It does not thereby become wiser, for wisdom is won by the individual through the particular work that he has performed and through the experience that he has gathered in the course of many incarnations and in a present life that has been lived to the full. It is very instructive to experience how naive or even foolish people who are over-clever can be, and how unwise those with brilliant gifts!

And how is it with the truth? It remains something to which mankind aspires. We never have it completely. What a lot of self-deception and delusion pours forth over it even when we think we are wholly in possession of it! How it is again and again torn into shreds through passion, self-righteousness, vanity and ambition! But if it lives as a striving, as a longing in the soul, there is always a foundation in the soul upon which one can build further, even if everything seems to be unsure. Then not everything is lost; one should not give way to despair. But even though it may have been stifled for a time, this longing must be present as a driving force within man, as a desire for the truth. If one lies cold-bloodedly, in full knowledge of the fact, and if such an impulse works consciously into the life of the community, it would be illusory to place any hopes upon its health.

Nevertheless, these are rare instances, and they must be verified by unshakeably firm facts if they are to count as such. The actual reality should never be clouded by an opinion that has been aroused through passion, by sympathy or by self-perpetuating rumours whipped up by emotion. Everything of this kind leads to fallacious conclusions.

What is there to be done if a community which bears within itself a holy obligation that has been taken on in the name of world history, which has a work to protect and further without which mankind will become utterly decadent, develops problems that it cannot solve internally? It wants to do justice to the obligation that has been laid upon it by destiny—and in spite of this it is unable to free itself from the chains and burdens which hinder it, because the individuals concerned are not able to overcome themselves. Blind discipleship does not, however, solve any problems. What is to be done? The resolve to *overcome oneself* should be consciously taken hold of by the community. Clearly and willingly.

We stand as a Society before the question of being or non-being. The catastrophes which have broken upon us through the World War, the isolation of countries, impoverishment etc. make it seem barely possible that we can preserve our identity as an external body, and yet miracles can still happen. They happen when the moral substance is of such strength that it can make a miracle possible. What can we do to rescue our moral substance?

We can forgive! Everyone can forgive what lies within him to forgive. We can forget what ought to be forgotten instead of rummaging about among old injustices. We could draw a line beneath all the old stories that wear us down and which, either because we are young or are no longer involved, we are not in a position to get to the bottom of. We can hold fast to the idea that what is fruitful is alone true. We must be able to work together again, in harmony and without excluding the people we do not like, preventing no one from participating who is true to the work and to Rudolf Steiner; without shutting ourselves off and barricading ourselves away from those who seek spiritual knowledge as only Rudolf Steiner can give it; without driving away the seeking souls for whose sake he consciously chose the path of martyrdom, out of love for mankind, for the whole of erring humanity. Love became knowledge in him—and it may become so also in us if we tread this path.

We stand before the twentieth anniversary of that fire which took his earthly life from him, even though for almost two years it continued to glow as a radiant sacrificial fire and brought us undreamt-of spiritual treasures through its flame. Can we not in view of this sacrifice and this death, for which we are surely all guilty both individually and as a Society—for he took *our* karma upon himself—can we not forget, become reconciled, and open our gates wide to those who seek them?

It seems to me that this offers us the only possibility for our purification—as a Society and as individuals. I say this in full awareness of the weightiness of these words, in awareness of the fact that in human estimation I shall shortly have to appear before Rudolf Steiner's spiritual form. Let us rescue his work and human culture by overcoming ourselves and achieving reconciliation, by opening our gates wide to those who seek them.

Marie Steiner

Appendix 2

The text of Ita Wegman's written answer to the 'Appeal'[*]

Ascona, 15 February '43
Kur-und Erholungsheim
Casa Andrea Cristoforo

Dear Frau Dr Steiner,

Please forgive my writing to you. I have read your Article to the Members, which you wrote shortly before Christmas 1942, in the Goetheanum supplement.

Your article can be read in so many different ways. I shall not permit myself to pass a judgement on it. I merely wish by means of these lines to let you know that your words made a deep impression on me; they are great and full of possibilities for the future.

For this I owe you, my dear Frau Dr Steiner, my thanks.

Yours respectfully
Ita Wegman

[*] Taken from *Marie Steiner. Briefe und Dokumente vornehmlich aus ihrem letzten Lebensjahr*, Dornach 1981.

Notes and Additions

All works by Rudolf Steiner are referred to by the *Gesamtausgabe* (GA) volume number from the catalogue of the collected edition of Rudolf Steiner's works in the original German (published by *Rudolf Steiner Verlag*, Dornach, Switzerland). For information on the published English language translations see the list on pages 196–99.

1. GA 4, chapter IX.
2. F. Rittelmeyer, *Das Vaterunser. Ein Weg zur Menschwerdung*, Stuttgart 1985. An English translation was published in 1931 under the title of *The Lord's Prayer*, but is now out of print.
3. Ibid.
4. Regarding the division of humanity into the two races of 'the good' and 'the evil' which is to begin in the sixth epoch, see the lecture of 25 June 1908 (GA 104).
5. See the description of 'Slavic man' in the paintings of the small cupola of the First Goetheanum in the lecture of 29 June 1921 (GA 290), also Appendix 1 to the present author's book *The Spiritual Origins of Eastern Europe and the Future Mysteries of the Holy Grail*, Temple Lodge 1993. See also H. Raske, *The Language of Colour in the First Goetheanum*, Dornach 1983. Regarding the relationship of Russian man to his double, see the lecture of 16 November 1917 (GA 178).
6. See note 157, and also the lecture of 25 June 1908 (GA 104).
7. See note 2.
8. See the lectures of 28 January 1907 (GA 96), 4 February and 6 March 1907 (GA 97).
9. Lecture of 4 February 1907 (GA 97).
10. Lecture of 28 January 1907 (GA 96).
11. See the lecture of 25 October 1918 (GA 185), and chapter VII.
12. See the lecture of 18 April 1909 (GA 110).

13. Lecture of 23 March 1915 (GA 174a).
14. See the lecture of 21 November 1911 (GA 132).
15. See GA 13, the chapter entitled 'Present and Future Evolution of the World and of Mankind'.
16. Ibid. Inasmuch as the greater periods of earthly evolution are reflected in the smaller, there is a connection between the future incarnation of Jupiter and the sixth great period of the Earth, which will begin after the 'War of all against All' (see note 6), and also the sixth cultural epoch (the Slavic). Moreover, the seven petitions of the Lord's Prayer are not only the keys to the seven cultural epochs but also to the seven great periods. Thus the earliest of these, the Polarian period, represents the expression of the *Will* of the spiritual world, guiding the earthly world to its physical manifestation. In the Hyperborean epoch, in the course of which the Sun separated from the Earth, the relationship to the Earth of the forces of the Sun *Kingdom* and the higher beings that inhabited it is conclusively defined. After the separation of the Moon in the Lemurian epoch, man appears for the first time in earthly evolution as a bearer of the divine *Name* (the individual ego). Then, on Atlantis, he finally appears on the Earth as a physical being. The problem of the 'daily bread' becomes for the first time a matter of some urgency. In the post-Atlantean period the problem of 'forgiveness'—as it is being considered in the present work—becomes fundamental for man. The sixth and seventh great periods will be marked by an ever-growing battle with evil, the conquest of which will be a necessity for the further spiritualizing of the Earth. The last two petitions of the Lord's Prayer are therefore key sayings for these periods. (A detailed characterization of the great periods that have been enumerated here is given in GA 11 and GA 13.)
17. Lecture of 6 February 1917 (GA 175).
18. Simon Wiesenthal, *die Sonnenblume. Eine Erzählung von Schuld und Vergebung*, Frankfurt 1984. In connection with the examples of forgiveness cited in this chapter, it should be borne in mind that the author felt compelled to limit himself to examples 'taken from life' and to exclude literary examples, inasmuch as their sheer abundance in world literature would have significantly increased the size of the book. In the works of the classical Russian authors (Tolstoy, Dostoevsky, Chekhov and so forth) and, in the twentieth century, especially in the writings of Albert Steffen, one can see how this theme has been deepened and developed in the form of art.

19. George G. Ritchie, Elizabeth Sherill, *Return from Tomorrow*, Kingsway Publications Ltd, Eastbourne 1978; originally published in the USA by Chosen Books 1978 and currently by Spire Books.

20. The letter is quoted according to its publication in the article 'Sobytiye 1 Marta i Vladamir Solovyov' in the 1988 edition (no. 11) of the magazine *Nashe Naslyediye* ('Our Heritage').

21. The draft of the letter is quoted according to the Complete Works of L.N. Tolstoy in 22 volumes, Moscow 1984, vol. 17, letter no. 378.

22. Alexander III's reaction to Solovyov's letter is contained in the article entitled 'The Event of 1 March' (see note 20), and to Tolstoy's in the notes to his second letter, printed as no. 380 (see note 21).

23. See further regarding this in the present author's book *The Spiritual Origins of Eastern Europe and the Future Mysteries of the Holy Grail*, parts II and III, Temple Lodge 1993.

24. *Nachrichtenblatt—Was in der Anthroposophischen Gesellschaftvorgeht*, published for members of the Anthroposophical Society as an appendix to the weekly *Das Goetheanum, Wochenschrift für Anthroposophie*. The text of 'Appeal for Reconciliation' is given in Appendix 1.

25. See *Marie Steiner, Briefe und Dokumente*, Dornach 1981, part III. Besides two further 'Appeals for Reconciliation' by Marie Steiner in 1943 and 1945, there was also in 1946 a suggestion to make the 'Nachlassverein a separate Section of the School of Spiritual Science' at the Goetheanum, all of which can be seen as the ongoing life of this impulse.

26. See the further text of Ita Wegman's letter in Appendix 2.

27. See Note 23.

28. Quoted in Marie Steiner's article 'Erinnerungsworte' ('Words of Recollection'), written in September 1926 and published in *Nachrichten der Rudolf Steiner Nachlassverwaltung* no. 23, Dornach 1968.

29. Lecture of 16 June 1923 (GA 258).

30. Rudolf Steiner also speaks about 'the fervent opposition ... which has indeed arisen with such vigour towards my intentions [in the Society]' in Stuttgart at a members' gathering on 4 September 1921 (see L. Kolisko, Eugen Kolisko, *Ein Lebensbild*, 1961).

31. See Note 28.

32. See *Marie Steiner, Briefe und Dokumente*, Dornach 1981, part I.

33. Quoted by E. Zeylmans, *Willem Zeylmans van Emmichoven. Ein Pionier der Anthroposophie*, Arlesheim 1979. The quotation that follows is from the same source.

34. See note 32.
35. 'The Close of the Year and the Turn of the Year'—Marie Steiner's Foreword to the first edition of the stenographical reports of the Christmas Conference (GA 260).
36. See note 33.
37. Ibid.
38. See Clara Kreutzer, *Starke Einheit in der freien Vielheit*, Stuttgart 1986, the chapter entitled 'Scheveninger Kreis'.
39. Lecture of 6 June 1907 (GA 99).
40. Lecture of 20 June 1912 (GA 133).
41. The special position of Christian Rosenkreutz—characterized in the words of Rudolf Steiner quoted above—as 'the greatest martyr among human beings', a position which results from his part in bearing the karma of the evolving individual human ego, was also reflected in that level of spiritual development which he attained after his initiation in 1459, as described in Valentin Andreae's book *The Chymical Wedding of Christian Rosenkreutz, anno 1459*. Moreover, the attainment of this higher stage was associated with that special initiation into 'the function of evil' which he received at this same time from Manes (see note 158).

     At the end of the *Chymical Wedding*, this stage of initiation is depicted in the image of Christian Rosenkreutz taking upon himself the task of the Guardian 'in his sky-blue habit', of him who stands at the sublime portal of the gates which divide the earthly world from the spiritual (in the imagination given by Rudolf Steiner to Ita Wegman, Christian Rosenkreutz appears in a blue garment. See pp. 37–38 and note 42). Christian Rosenkreutz accomplishes this deed willingly and he characterizes it as follows: 'I thought that nothing could be more worthy than to demonstrate some noble virtue in honour of my order; and there was at that time none which seemed to me so laudable and so utterly wretched as gratitude. Thus although I might well have wished for something more agreeable to myself, I overcame my reservations and decided, wholly disregarding the peril to which I was subjected, to free the Guardian, my benefactor.'* In

---

* *Translator's footnote.* English versions of the *Chymical Wedding* may be found in *The Chymical Wedding of Christian Rosenkreutz*, Minerva Books, London, and *A Commentary on The Chymical Wedding of Christian Rosenkreutz* by Margaret Bennell and Isobel Wyatt, Temple Lodge, London 1989. See also Paul M. Allen, *A Christian Rosenkreutz Anthology*, Steiner Books, NY 1981.

these words we may again find both the principal elements of true forgiveness: the overcoming of self and the sacrificial giving of oneself to the world, which makes possible the liberation of humanity. Then the *Chymical Wedding* goes on to say that the fulfilment of such a sacrifice and taking on such a difficult task was no easy matter even for so advanced an individuality as Christian Rosenkreutz, and demanded from him a real struggle.

In order that we may really understand the significance of the task of the *Guardian of humanity* that Christian Rosenkreutz has taken upon himself, we need to turn to Rudolf Steiner's lecture of 27 March 1913 (GA 145). There we find a description of how with the conscious crossing of the threshold the heavenly *counter-image* of what is related in the Old Testament through the story of Cain and Abel is revealed to the initiate. The substance of this counter-image is that the initiate must fully unite in the spiritual worlds with his higher spiritual principle (the higher ego), which appears there as an independent spiritual being. And as this higher spiritual being is at the same time the embodiment of absolute sacrifice, a union with it can be achieved by the initiate only through a step similar to that taken by Christian Rosenkreutz.

This step consists in that, having united with this spiritual being, Christian Rosenkreutz did not remain in the spiritual world but, under the guidance of the higher inspirations which can be compared to those originating from the Greater Guardian of the Threshold, descended again to the Earth (see last chapter of GA 13) in order *there* to become the Guardian of this being within man, that is, the Guardian of the evolution of the higher ego within humanity. In the above lecture, Rudolf Steiner describes the inspiration that the initiate receives at such a moment in the following words: 'Because you have found the way to the other [spiritual being] and have united yourself with his bounteous sacrifice, you may now return to Earth with him, in him, and I will make you his guardian on Earth.' Thus as a result of his initiation in 1459, Christian Rosenkreutz attained a pole in his individual development that was diametrically opposite to that occupied by Cain at the very beginning of the earthly evolution of mankind. In those distant times, Cain gave the following answer to this voice of higher inspiration: 'Am I my brother's keeper?' (Genesis 4:9). With this he necessarily directed the subsequent evolution of humanity towards the development of the individual earthly ego and towards the ever-growing alienation of human beings—even to the eventual possibility of the 'War of All against All' arising among them—that derives from it. In contrast to this, Christian Rosenkreutz willingly became the 'guardian' of his human brothers and sisters in their endeavour to develop within themselves the higher ego, which leads to the future union of human beings in a new spiritual-social whole (see further regarding this in S.O. Prokofieff, *The Cycle of the Year as a Path of Initiation Leading to an Experience of the Christ Being*, part IV, ch. 6, Temple Lodge 1995).

One can also say that, in becoming the 'guardian' of evolving humanity, Christian Rosenkreutz—in a certain sense—at the same time takes upon himself the karma of Cain, or to be more precise, the karma of the ego-development of mankind that was the consequence of his deed, in order gradually to direct it—in the spirit of Manichaeism—towards the good. In the language of the starry script, this mission of Christian Rosenkreutz can be characterized as the gradual transformation of the forces of the Scorpion into the forces of the Eagle.

42. See M. and E. Kirchner-Bockholt, *Rudolf Steiner's Mission and Ita Wegman*, privately printed 1977, the chapter entitled 'Rudolf Steiner's Mission'.
43. See S.O. Prokofieff, *Rudolf Steiner and the Founding of the New Mysteries*, Temple Lodge 1994.
44. GA 13, the chapter entitled 'The Nature of Humanity'.
45. Ibid.
46. Lecture of 8 February 1924 (GA 234).
47. Lecture of 10 February 1924 (GA 234).
48. Lecture of 26 June 1924 (GA 317).
49. In the lecture of 20 February 1917 (GA 175), Rudolf Steiner formulates this thought as follows: 'So that instead of using the complicated expression, "We are in connection with the Hierarchy of the Angeloi", we can simply say: "We are in connection with what is to come in the future—our Spirit Self".'
50. See GA 15, chapter III.
51. GA 93a.
52. Lecture of 8 August 1920 (GA 199).
53. GA 26, the article entitled 'The World-Thoughts in the Working of Michael and in the Working of Ahriman' (16 November 1924).
54. GA 10, chapter entitled 'Conditions'.
55. Lecture of 11 February 1919 (GA 193). Rudolf Steiner also speaks about the need of developing *tolerance* on the path of modern spirit-

pupilship in GA 10, in connection with the development of the twelve-petalled lotus flower (see the chapter entitled 'Some Effects of Initiation').

56. Ibid, also the following quotation.

57. Lecture of 1 January 1919 (GA 187).

58. Lecture of 20 May 1912 (GA 133). If, as Rudolf Steiner says, the appearance of Christ in the etheric sphere which has its beginning in the twentieth century is going to last three thousand years, its end, and at the same time its culmination, will come around AD 4900– 5000, which will correspond to the second half of the sixth cultural epoch (AD 3573–5733).

59. This rests upon the fact that, while in a true process of forgiveness it is the forces of Manas (the Spirit Self) which participate, in the process of taking upon oneself the karma of others it is the forces of Buddhi (the Life Spirit)—which in our time can be attained only on the path of spirit-pupilship (see the lecture of 24 October 1905, GA 93a).

60. Lecture of 4 November 1904 (GA 93).

61. Rudolf Steiner says in this connection: 'Progress will be made in this direction only when human beings develop a heightened intellectual power not merely for themselves but also raise it up into the astral world. Through such an intellectual clairvoyance, the etherically visible Christ can and will approach a human being who has advanced in this way more and more clearly in the course of the next three thousand years'. Lecture of 18 November 1911 (GA 130).

62. Rudolf Steiner describes the two latter stages as the meetings with the Greater Guardian (see GA 10) and with the Christ in Intuition (see GA 13).

63. Lecture of 21 September 1911 (GA 130).

64. See the lecture of 18 April 1909 (GA 110).

65. Ibid.

66. GA 14, *The Guardian of the Threshold*, Scene 8. The next quotation is from the same source.

67. In trying to seize hold of man's inner being and asserting their authority over him, the opposing powers are pursuing one further purpose. It is as follows: what in life is man's inner nature becomes after his death, as a result of a process of 'turning inside out', the whole planetary cosmos (see, for example, the lecture of 28 August 1923, GA 223). And from this the possibility emerges for the opposing powers to extend the authority which they have gained over man over the whole cosmos as well.

68. See note 70. The relationship of the astral body with the Moon and the etheric body with the Sun stems from the fact that the rudiments of the first of these were formed within man on Old Moon and of the second on Old Sun. See also GA 13, the chapter entitled 'The Evolution of the World and of Man'.

69. Rudolf Steiner says in this connection: 'The ego [of man] could only appear on Earth in bodies that were sufficiently prepared for it and then develop further under the nurturing influences of the Christ-impulse, because Christ is on a macrocosmic scale what our ego is—and signifies for us human beings—on a microcosmic scale' (lecture of 18 November 1911, GA 130). And then, in another lecture: 'Thus it was altogether in accordance with the evolution of the Christ Being, once He had descended to our Earth from the macrocosm, to bring the great impulse from the macrocosmic Ego, so that the microcosmic ego, the human ego, might receive this impulse and take a further step in its evolution' (lecture of 9 January 1912, GA 130). Regarding Christ as the new Spirit of the Earth, see the lecture of 26 May 1908 (GA 103).

70. Regarding the Resurrection body or 'Phantom', see the lectures of 10 and 11 October 1911 (GA 121). Rudolf Steiner characterizes the luciferic beings as having remained behind on Old Moon and as belonging originally to the Hierarchy of the Angels, and the ahrimanic beings as having remained behind on Old Sun, which is to say that they belonged to the Hierarchy of the Archangels. (See, for example, the lecture of 22 May 1910, GA 120.) The Asuras he characterizes as beings who remained behind on Old Saturn and as belonging to the Hierarchy of the Archai or the Spirits of Personality. (See the lecture of 2 June 1907, GA 99.) In this connection, in answer to a question about the Asuras on 21 April 1909 (GA 110), Rudolf Steiner says: 'The Asuras—the evil ones—are beings who are one degree higher in their will towards evil than the ahrimanic beings and two degrees higher than the luciferic.'

In order that we may better understand this process of the redemption of these three categories of opposing spirits, it is necessary for us briefly to characterize the nature of the rightly evolved spirits corresponding to them, that is, the Angels, Archangels and Archai. As we know, the Angels are the bearers of a fully evolved Spirit Self, their outermost sheath is the etheric body and their highest member, the eighth, is *above* the Spirit Man. The Archangels bear within themselves a fully evolved Life Spirit, their outermost sheath is the astral body and their highest member is the ninth. The Archai bear within themselves a fully evolved Spirit Man, their lowest member corresponds to the human ego and their highest is the tenth. These three highest members, the eighth, ninth and tenth, which form the highest ideal of beings of the Third Hierarchy, just as the highest ideal of earthly humanity is the attainment of the stage of Spirit Man (the seventh member), are known in Christian esotericism as the Holy Spirit, the Son and the Father (see regarding this the lecture of 2 June 1907, GA 99). (Naturally, this is not the 'Absolute' Trinity itself but only its reflection on a higher cosmic plane.)

From this it follows that the Angels are beings who in their Spirit Self are constantly living in Imaginations of the Holy Spirit that the Archangels are in their Life Spirit filled with Inspirations of the Son, and the Archai, in their Spirit Man, with Intuitions of the Father. Thus they may be seen as the servants and ambassadors of the Holy Trinity in the spiritual world.

In the same way, the retarded Angels, Archangels and Archai also bear within themselves respectively an evolved Spirit Self, Life Spirit and Spirit Man. But the relationship of these spiritual members with the higher Trinity (that is, with the eighth, ninth and tenth members) has been broken off. Thus Lucifer does not aspire out of his Spirit Self to his eighth member but rather turns away from it and so becomes the antagonist of the Holy Spirit in the cosmos. Similarly, Ahriman averts his eyes from his ninth member and becomes the adversary of the Son (Christ), while the Asuras, in turning away from the tenth member, become the opponents of the Father.

Only through having recounted this can we understand more deeply the process of their redemption (as described above). For as they encounter the Spirit Self of Christ—which bears within itself the forces of the Holy Spirit—in man's astral body, the luciferic beings again find a rightful relationship with their eighth, and highest, member, and through it also with the lawful or good cosmos, which is in its origins essentially a reflection of the Holy Trinity. Then, as they encounter Christ's Life Spirit—which bears within itself the forces of the Son—in man's etheric body, the ahrimanic spirits find once again a relationship with their ninth, and highest, member and through it with the good cosmos. And, finally, the Asuras, as they encounter in man's physical body the 'substance of the Risen One' which issues from Christ's Spirit Man, the bearer of the forces of the Father, acquire a new relationship to their tenth member, and through it again enter into the life of the good cosmos. In other words, they again turn towards the forces of the higher Trinity and become its servants, just like all the other rightly evolved Hierarchies.

At the end of chapter VIII, something will be said about the actual path arising out of Anthroposophy whereby man can even now learn to participate in this process of redemption.

71. GA 107.

72. See lectures of 22 March 1909 (GA 107) and 23 May 1904 (GA 93), and also Note 70.

73. See the lecture of 31 August 1909 (GA 113). Rudolf Steiner speaks about the work of true Rosicrucians for the redemption of Lucifer in the lecture of 28 August 1909 (ibid.). In still earlier times this work was carried out in the esoteric circles of the Grail Mystery, and the legend about the precious stone from which the Holy Chalice was formed as being from the crown of Lucifer is an indication of this (see the lectures of 23 and 27 August 1909, ibid.).

74. Lecture of 22 March 1909 (GA 107). There is an ancient manuscript, the original of which is kept in the Vatican Library and is one of its most treasured secrets, which tells of Lucifer's redemption and also of the Mystery of Pentecost (which is associated with it). The only person who possessed a copy of it was the Count of Saint-Germain in the eighteenth century (see the lecture of 23 May 1904, GA 93).

75. Lecture of 22 March 1909 (GA 107).

76. See, for example, the final monologue of Benedictus in the fourth Mystery Play, *The Soul's Awakening* (GA 14).

77. Rudolf Steiner speaks in the following lectures about the earthly incarnation of Ahriman, which is due to take place at the beginning of the third Christian millennium: 1 and 15 November 1919 (GA 191); 27 October and 4 November 1919 (GA 193); and 28 December 1919 (GA 195).

78. See note 75.

79. This enables us to understand why Rudolf Steiner says so little about the Asuras. In the first place, this is because their temptation is still a future prospect for humanity (see note 75), and in the second place because the potential for withstanding them will be directly dependent upon the direction that earthly evolution will take as a result of the imminent incarnation of Ahriman; in other words, upon the extent to which humanity will be spiritually prepared for his

coming and for overcoming those mighty temptations that will issue from him.

80. That the sevenfold path of initiation is of a Rosicrucian nature Rudolf Steiner affirms in GA 13, and in many of his earlier lectures. See, for example, 11 December 1906 (GA 97) and 6 June 1907 (GA 99).

81. *The Guardian of the Threshold*, scene 6 (GA 14). In the lecture of 9 April 1924 (GA 240), Rudolf Steiner illustrates this law by means of the karmic connection between Garibaldi, who in his past incarnation had been a priest of the Hibernian Mysteries, and three of his pupils from that time, who in the nineteenth century incarnated as Cavour, Mazzini and King Victor Emmanuel.

82. See further regarding this sixth stage in S.O. Prokofieff, *The Cycle of the Year as a Path of Initiation Leading to an Experience of the Christ Being*, part X, chapter 2, Temple Lodge 1995.

83. For this reason, Rudolf Steiner in his many descriptions of the sevenfold Rosicrucian path of initiation hardly ever speaks about its seventh, and highest, stage, which in his early lectures he calls 'Divine Bliss' (see note 80), and in GA 13, more generally, 'the combined experience of what has been already learnt as a basic soul-mood'.

84. See the full text of the 'Appeal' in Appendix 1.

85. The future transformation of conscience into the new faculty of clairvoyantly beholding the consequences of one's own deeds will be a significant help on this path (see the lecture of 8 May 1910, GA 116). This metamorphosis of conscience is directly associated with the appearance of Christ in the etheric realm. Human beings will then be able to behold clairvoyantly—as a karmic vision—what they have to accomplish in their lives so as to strengthen the forces of good on Earth in the sense of the Manichaean principle (the transformation of evil into good). In this way they will become the collaborators of Christ Himself in the process of the transformation of karma.

86. GA 10, the chapter entitled 'Initiation'.

87. Ibid.

88. See the lecture of 19 November 1922 (GA 218).

89. Lecture of 13 January 1924 (GA 233).

90. See the lecture of 27 January 1908 (GA 102), and S.O. Prokofieff, *The Twelve Holy Nights and the Spiritual Hierarchies*, Temple Lodge 1993.

91. Rudolf Steiner employs this expression in the article entitled 'The Michael-Christ Experience of Man' (2 November 1924, GA 26).

92. Lecture of 8 June 1924 (GA 239).
93. GA 13, the chapter entitled 'Present and Future Evolution of the World and of Humanity'.
94. See the lectures of 14 October 1911 (GA 131) and 2 December 1911 (GA 130).
95. See the lecture of 2 December 1911 (GA 130).
96. Lecture of 21 September 1911 (GA 130).
97. Lecture of 8 May 1910 (GA 116); see also the lecture of 14 October 1911 (GA 130).
98. See, for example, the lecture of 26 May 1908 (GA 103); 7 July 1909 (GA 112); 26 September 1909 (GA 114); and 15–16 July 1914 (GA 155).
99. GA 104 and GA 13, chapter entitled 'Present and Future Evolution of the World and of Humanity'.
100. Lecture of 15 July 1914 (GA 155).
101. Ibid.
102. Ibid.
103. Lecture of 19 March (GA 181).
104. Lecture of 24 March 1908 (GA 102); see also chapter VI, part 5.
105. The full definition of the Spirit Self in GA 9 runs as follows: 'The spirit sends its rays into the ego and lives in it as in a "sheath". This spirit which forms an ego and lives as an ego will be called the "Spirit Self", because it manifests as the ego or "selfhood" within man.' And: 'The Spirit Self is a *revelation* of the spiritual world within the ego.' These words relate above all to the working of the Spirit Self during the *present* incarnation of the Earth, where its forces are able to manifest themselves within man only as a revelation from above. Nevertheless, this 'revelation of the Spirit Self' is not something abstract but is associated with the actual entering of its substance into the ego. Moreover, the word 'revelation' in this case is an indication that the Spirit Self is at this stage not as yet a *property of man*, that his ego is not yet *completely* encompassed by it—as will be the situation on Jupiter—but that it merely 'overshines' the human ego 'from above', while its essential being remains in the spiritual world (see the lecture of 20 February 1917, GA 175).

This process can also be characterized by means of the words where Rudolf Steiner depicts the descending of the Spirit Self in the sixth cultural epoch: 'Thus when, in the course of the sixth cultural epoch, the Spirit Self will enter into human beings a spiritual Sun will indeed be present towards which all people will incline and in which they will find harmony ... This sixth cultural epoch will be a very important one; for it will bring peace and brotherhood through a common wisdom. Peace and brotherhood, because not only will the higher self—initially in its lower form, as the Spirit Self or Manas [the higher forms meant here are the Life Spirit and Spirit Man]—descend for certain chosen individuals but also for that part of humanity passing through a normal evolution. A union of the human ego as it has gradually evolved with the higher, unifying ego will then take place. We can call this a *spiritual marriage*—which was also the name given in Christian esotericism to the union of the human ego with Manas or the Spirit Self' (lecture of 30 May 1908, GA 103).

106. Regarding the inner relationship of the Holy Spirit to the human principle of the Spirit Self, see—for example—the lecture of 25 March 1907 (GA 96).

107. Lecture of 16 July 1914 (GA 155).

108. See the lectures of 9 November 1914 (GA 158) and 3 December 1914 (GA 174a).

109. Lecture of 9 November 1914 (as above).

110. Lecture of 16 November 1917 (GA 178).

111. Lecture of 9 November 1914 (GA 158).

112. Lecture of 16 October 1918 (GA 182).

113. See S.O. Prokofieff: *The Spiritual Origins of Eastern Europe and the Future Mysteries of the Holy Grail*, part III, chapter 20, Temple Lodge 1993.

114. See the lecture of 2 November 1908 (GA 107).

115. See the lecture of 4 February 1913 (GA 144).

116. Lecture of 14 August 1917 (GA 176).

117. Lecture of 4 June 1924 (GA 236).

118. Ibid.

119. See the lecture of 2 November 1908 (GA 107).

120. See lecture of 26 August 1923 (GA 227).

121. Subsequently, still closer to the Turning Point of Time, it was generally only evil Gods (luciferic and ahrimanic) who 'remembered' mankind. Hence the idea of the 'envy of the Gods' which was widespread in late antiquity (see the lecture of 31 December 1923, GA 233).

122. For example, the voice of the 'Bath-Kol' (mentioned in Jewish occultism) in the original, undistorted form in which it inspired the prophet Elijah. Rudolf Steiner speaks about it in the lecture of 5 October 1913 (GA 148).

123. Lecture of 2 May 1910 (GA 116).
124. Lecture of 8 May 1910 (GA 116).
125. Quoted in a lecture of Carl Unger entitled 'Was ist Anthro-posophie?', collected works of Carl Unger in 3 volumes; vol. 1, Stuttgart 1964.
126. In the text of the 'Macrocosmic Lord's Prayer' the last line runs: 'Ye Fathers in the heavens'. According to Rudolf Steiner, by the word 'Fathers' is meant the entire company of the divine-spiritual Hier-archies that rule mankind. See lectures of 20 September 1913 (GA 245) and 17 December 1913 (GA 148).
127. This element of knowledge with respect to all that is evil and imperfect in the world has an important part to play in modern spirit-pupilship. Rudolf Steiner writes in this connection in GA 10: 'The pupil suppresses all superfluous criticism of whatever is imperfect, evil and wrong and tries rather to understand everything that comes to him.'
128. See the lectures of 16 January 1916 (GA 165) and 27 August 1924 (GA 240).
129. See the spiritual-scientific commentaries of Rudolf Steiner on the Lord's Prayer in the lectures of 28 January 1907 (GA 96) and 4 February and 6 March 1907 (GA 97).
130. Lecture of 15 June 1915 (GA 159/160).
131. Lecture of 2 October 1913 (GA 148).
132. Lecture of 24 March 1908 (GA 102).
133. This condition is also a highly important part of the modern path of spirit-pupilship. In GA 10, Rudolf Steiner refers to it as the second condition of pupilship, one that is associated with the etheric body, and formulates it as follows: 'The second condition is to feel oneself *a member* of humanity as a whole.' And then he goes on to speak about the need for the following feeling to arise within the pupil: '... that I am only a member of humanity as a whole and *share responsibility* for everything that occurs.' (In both cases the italics are in the original.)
134. Lecture of 7 December 1918 (GA 186).
135. Rudolf Steiner speaks on several occasions in his lectures about the possibilities of preparing already in our time for the Spirit Self (sixth) epoch in human evolution. See, for instance, the lectures of 7 February 1913 (GA 144) and 15 June 1915 (GA 159/160).
136. See the lectures of 30 May 1908 (GA 103) and 20 June 1908 (GA 104).
137. Lecture of 11 September 1910 (GA 123). The quotations that follow are from the same source.

138. See the lecture of 25 June 1908 (GA 104).
139. Lecture of 23 November 1919 (GA 194).
140. Lecture of 8 August 1924 (GA 237).
141. Lecture of 15 September 1922 (GA 215).
142. See S.O. Prokofieff, *Rudolf Steiner and the Founding of the New Mysteries*, Temple Lodge 1994, part III, chapter 7.
143. See the text of the 'Appeal' in Appendix 1 to the present work.
144. Lecture of 11 June 1922 (GA 211).
145. Lecture of 15 June 1915 (GA 159/160).
146. Lecture of 25 October 1918 (GA 185).
147. Ibid. The next quotation is from the same source.
148. Lecture of 2 May 1913 (GA 152). [A large part of the extract quoted by the author does not appear in the English edition—*Occult Science and Occult Development*, Rudolf Steiner Press 1966—or in the German edition on which it is based, and can be found only in the German edition of August 1980—Translator's note.]
149. Lecture of 26 October 1918 (GA 185).
150. In the lecture of 26 October 1918 (GA 185), Rudolf Steiner says in this connection: 'He who crosses the threshold of the spiritual world discovers that there is not a single crime to which every person, in so far as he belongs to the fifth post-Atlantean epoch, is not subconsciously prone. Whether in any particular case this inclination towards evil leads outwardly to an evil action depends not upon this inclination but upon altogether different factors.'
151. In the lecture of 6 February 1917 (GA 175), Rudolf Steiner speaks about modern spiritual science as the spiritual *language* in which the humanity of the present and the future will be able to turn to the Etheric Christ; similarly in the lecture of 1 October 1911 (GA 130), he indicates that the union of the two streams of etherized blood (flowing within man from the heart to the head) which leads to a clairvoyant experience of the Etheric Christ can take place now only through a real *understanding* of the Christ-impulse, as this is now given to humanity in spiritual science.
152. Lecture of 26 October 1918 (GA 185).
153. See the lecture of 22 March 1909 (GA 107).
154. See the description of the Rosicrucian meditation in GA 13, the chapter entitled 'Knowledge of Higher Worlds', and also the 'Grail Meditation' in the lecture of 6 June 1907 (GA 99).
155. The beginning of this gradual overcoming of death among mankind—at any rate in its modern form—will also have a correspon-

dence in a completely different process of birth. Rudolf Steiner refers to this in the lecture of 28 October 1917 (GA 177), and relates the time of its diffusion on Earth to the seventh cultural epoch.

156. The process of 'moral breathing' can be enacted already at the preceding stage of the Manichaean path of initiation described in this book. It begins through the powers of *understanding* and *tolerance* towards the thoughts and views of other people being gradually brought to a focus in the capacity to—so to speak—'inhale' the materialistic thoughts of modern civilization and 'exhale' spiritual thoughts. This, among much else, is one of the most important tasks of anthroposophists in our time. Rudolf Steiner in his own life presented an archetypal example of this process: having 'inhaled' Haeckel's theory of evolution into his soul, he lifted it up into the spiritual world by means of the methods of initiation which he described and then 'exhaled' it as the all-embracing picture of world evolution described in *Occult Science* (GA 13) (see the lecture of 13 January 1924, GA 233a).

157. What is meant here are not the cultural epochs but the great periods, each of which embraces seven smaller periods, corresponding to the successive cultures. To such great periods belong those such as the Polarian, Hyperborean, Lemurian, Atlantean, the present post-Atlantean and, following or after it, the sixth.

158. Lecture of 11 November 1904 (GA 93). The next quotation is from the same source. What is said here is further confirmed by the fact that, according to Rudolf Steiner, Manes himself initiated Christian Rosenkreutz in 1459 into the Manichaean Mysteries of the knowledge of evil (see the 'Barr Manuscript', in GA 262).

159. Lecture of 25 June 1908 (GA 104).

160. In his book *Knowledge of the Higher Worlds* Rudolf Steiner speaks about the significance of precisely this soul quality also for the modern Christian–Rosicrucian path of pupilship, characterizing 'gentleness' as 'one of the main factors in all esoteric training', one which 'opens one's inner [spiritual] eyes' (see the chapter entitled 'Practical Aspects').

161. There is, according to the spiritual–scientific research of Rudolf Steiner, a direct relationship between the founder of Manichaeism, who lived in the third century, and Parsifal, who lived in the period straddling the eighth and ninth centuries—namely, that Parsifal is one of the subsequent incarnations of Manes (see GA 264).

162. Rudolf Steiner speaks in this connection in the lecture of 16 July

1914 (GA 155): 'Let us bring all this together, my dear friends, and reflect from this point of view upon the words with which Christ sent His disciples out into the world to proclaim His name and, in His name, to forgive sins. Why to forgive sins in His name? Because the forgiveness of sins is connected with His name . . .' Only in two Gospels, those of St Luke and St John, is the gift of forgiveness of sins mentioned in the scene of the Apostles being sent out by the Risen One; in the first of the two this gift is linked to the *name* of Christ (24, 27), and in the second with the Holy Spirit who was sent by Him (20, 22–23). Thus one can say: Luke describes more the outer aspect of the event, as he speaks of the forgiving of sins through the power of the Spirit Self (the name) of Christ, while John points to the esoteric aspect—he describes the Spirit Self of Christ as the revelation of the Holy Spirit (see also note 70).

163. Lecture of 7 February 1913 (GA 144).

164. Regarding those two paths to Christ, the starting point of one of which is tolerance and the other, the new idealism, see the lecture of 11 February 1919 (GA 193). And for the Rosicrucian path as a path of initiation for the *will*, see the lecture of 19 June 1908 (GA 104).

165. Lecture of 11 November 1904 (GA 93). The quotation that follows is from the same source.

166. See further in *The Cycle of the Year as a Path of Initiation*, Temple Lodge 1995, part XII, chapters 2 and 3.

167. See the lecture of 6 February 1917 (GA 175).

168. Lecture of 13 January 1924 (GA 233a).

169. Ibid.

170. See Matthew 5:39–41, 44; 18:21–22; Luke 6:29, 27–28, 35, 37.

171. Lecture of 11 November 1904 (GA 93).

172. Quoted from Fernand Niel, *Albigeois et Cathares*, Presses Universitaires de France, Paris 1959.

173. Lecture of 11 November 1904 (GA 93).

174. Regarding the esoteric council summoned by Manes in the fourth century, in which not only he but also Scythianos, Zarathustra and Buddha participated, see the lecture of 31 August 1909 (GA 113); regarding the initiation of Christian Rosenkreutz in the thirteenth century, see the lecture of 27 September 1911 (GA 130); and regarding the Rosicrucians as the guardians of the Grail Mysteries in modern times, the lecture of 24 June 1909 (GA 112). (See also note 80 and GA 13, where the modern Rosicrucian path of initiation is

characterized as leading to 'knowledge of the Grail' and where its initiates are called 'initiates of the Grail'.)

175. Rudolf Steiner speaks in the lecture of 31 August 1909 (GA 113), about the participants in the council of the fourth century (see note 174) being the principal esoteric teachers in the schools of true Rosicrucians (see also the lecture of 31 May 1909, GA 109).

176. Lecture of 25 June 1908 (GA 104).

177. See the lectures of 14 October 1911 (GA 131) and 2 December 1911 (GA 130).

178. GA 28. The next two quotations are from the same source.

179. See *Human and Cosmic Thought* (GA 151). Rudolf Steiner later both spoke and wrote on several occasions about the need for a conscious development of this faculty on the path of modern spirit pupilship. For example, in GA 10, we read: 'The pupils are enjoined to listen at certain times, by way of practice, to the most contradictory views and to silence in themselves all positive agreement and, more especially, all adverse criticism.' (From the chapter entitled 'Preparation'.)

180. GA 28.

181. See the lecture of 4 November 1913 (GA 148) and S.O. Prokofieff, *Rudolf Steiner and the Founding of the New Mysteries*, Temple Lodge 1994.

182. The faculty of perceiving the higher ego of another person, that is, following his soul after death in full consciousness, was the result of the occult teaching that Rudolf Steiner received at that time from his esoteric teacher. According to his own testimony, the starting-point for the occult teaching that he received at that time was the works of Fichte, the philosopher of the 'ego'.

183. GA 28. The quotations that follow are from the same source.

184. GA 28, chapter XVIII; the 'Barr Manuscript' (GA 262) and also the reference to Nietzsche and Haeckel in the karma lectures of 15 and 23 March 1924 (GA 235).

185. See also what is said about Nietzsche and Haeckel in the lectures of 20 July 1924 (GA 240) and 13 January 1924 (GA 233).

186. Lecture of 23 September 1924 (GA 238).

187. See the so-called 'Hague Conversation', published in *W.J. Stein/ Rudolf Steiner. Dokumentation eines wegweisenden Zusammenwirkens*, Dornach, 1985.

188. See Friedrich Rittelmeyer, *Rudolf Steiner Enters My Life*, Floris Books 1963 (translation by D.S. Osmond).

189. From a letter to W. Hübbe-Schleiden, published in *Briefe Rudolf Steiners*, vol. 2, Dornach, 1953.
190. The 'Barr Manuscript' in GA 262.
191. *Mitteilungen für Mitglieder der Deutschen Sektion der Theosophischen Gesellschaft*, no. XIV, December 1912.
192. See GA 28, chapter XXXI.
193. See Friedrich Rittelmeyer, *Rudolf Steiner Enters My Life*, Floris Books 1963.
194. F. Poeppig, *Rückblick auf Erlebnisse, Begegnungen und Persönlichkeiten in der anthroposophischen Bewegung 1923–1963*, Basel 1964.
195. See Note 193 (likewise the next quotation).
196. Quoted in Christoph Lindenberg, *Rudolf Steiner. Eine Chronik*, Stuttgart 1988.
197. See S.O. Prokofieff, *Rudolf Steiner and the Founding of the New Mysteries*, Temple Lodge 1994, parts I and II.
198. GA 262, letter no. 210.
199. See Friedrich Rittelmeyer, *Rudolf Steiner Enters my Life*, Floris Books, 1963.
200. The Memoirs of Max Hayek were first published in April 1925 in *Östereichische Blätter für freies Geistesleben*.
201. See p. 32. We can find a higher archetype in the events of Palestine also for his deed of becoming united with the 'inner opposition' within the Society. According to the Fifth Gospel, Christ Jesus did not fully overcome Ahriman in the third temptation, where the devil showed Him the full extent of his power right into the social sphere, but He consciously allowed him to remain beside Him. This was necessary in order that His mission might be fulfilled, for by remaining beside Him, Ahriman could then work through Judas (see the lecture of 18 November 1913, GA 148). Through this deed, Christ Jesus also completely broke with the traditions and the occult practice of the Essenes, who strove at all cost—even at the cost of other people—to keep the ahrimanic forces at a distance from themselves (see the lecture of 5 October 1913, GA 148).
202. GA 10, the chapter entitled 'Life and Death. The Greater Guardian of the Threshold'.
203. See 'The Close of the Year and the Turn of the Year'—Marie Steiner's Foreword, in GA 260.
204. 'Words of Remembrance for Charlotte Ferreri and Edith Maryon', Dornach, 3 May 1924 (GA 261).
205. In her article 'In Memory of the Christmas Foundation Meeting' of

26 April 1925, Ita Wegman recalls in this connection: 'Then the master felt ill. At first it was merely physical exhaustion, but then it became apparent that the illness had deeper causes, that karma was taking its toll. From January 1925 onwards he did not speak any longer of exhaustion but rather of the working of karma' (*An die Freunde*, Arlesheim 1960). See also her article of 7 June 1925. Marie Steiner likewise speaks of this in certain places. See notes 28 and 35, and the text of her 'Appeal' in Appendix 1.

206. See Friedrich Rittelmeyer, *Rudolf Steiner Enters My Life*, Floris Books 1963.
207. See Appendix 1.
208. After the Christmas Conference, Rudolf Steiner speaks about this as follows: 'One cannot enter the Anthroposophical Society—at least, one cannot enter it in a thoroughly sincere way that really moves the soul—without being deeply and fundamentally influenced in one's destiny.' Lecture of 3 August 1924 (GA 237).
209. GA 260, 'On behalf of the Members'.
210. In the lecture of 27 April 1924 (GA 236) Rudolf Steiner speaks of how the very contemplation of the forms of the First Goetheanum was to facilitate in the beholder the arising of a direct perception of karmic relationships.
211. See S.O. Prokofieff, *Rudolf Steiner and the Founding of the New Mysteries*, Temple Lodge 1994.
212. Lecture of 16 October 1918 (GA 182); the next quotation is from the same source.
213. Respectively, GA 28 and GA 13. See also S.O. Prokofieff, *Rudolf Steiner and the Founding of the New Mysteries*, Temple Lodge 1994.
214. Rudolf Steiner speaks in a number of lectures about the incarnation of Lucifer in Asia in the third millennium before Christ, the result of which was an intense 'luciferization' of the whole of eastern wisdom (see note 77).
215. Lecture of 27 November 1916 (GA 172).
216. Lecture of 18 October 1915 (GA 254). Annie Besant maintained the same line. This can be seen from the very title of her principal book on Christianity, *Esoteric Christianity or the Lesser Mysteries* (Theosophical Publishing House, Illinois 1970). There—in comparison with esoteric Christianity, which she calls the 'lesser Mysteries'—she characterizes the pre-Christian (Eastern) Mysteries (which have a luciferic character) as the 'greater'. In the same book there is also that fatal error—the confusing of Christ Jesus with Jeshu ben Pandira

(who lived a century earlier)—which served as the foundation for the whole affair of the Indian boy Krishnamurti-Alcyone (see GA 28, chapter XXXI). Thus when Annie Besant suggested to Rudolf Steiner that he take the above-mentioned book as the basis for the work with the German section of the Theosophical Society, this was decisively rejected by him.

217. See the lecture of 18 October 1915 (GA 254) and also the 'Barr Manuscript' (in GA 262).

218. See p. 67 ff.

219. See note 77.

220. Already in the first article of the magazine *Lucifer* (later *Lucifer-Gnosis*) which he edited in Berlin, an article which was published in June 1903 under the same title and had the aim of characterizing the entire spiritual direction of the magazine, Rudolf Steiner endeavoured to show that man has an obligation to create a *counterweight* to this spirit in his soul through his connection with the Christ-impulse. (See GA 34, and the lecture of 18 October 1915, in GA 254.)

221. Lecture of 21 September 1918 (GA 184). The next quotation is from the same source.

222. Heinz Müller, *Spuren auf dem Weg. Erinnerungen*, Stuttgart 1976. The next quotation is also taken from this book.

223. Lecture of 7 December 1918 (GA 186).

224. Related by Willi Aeppli at the beginning of the gathering to mark the sixtieth anniversary of the Engelberg Branch. Reported to the author by Rex Raab.

225. Lecture of 29 June 1921 (GA 290).

226. See, for example, the lectures of 17 October 1905 (GA 93a) and 2 June 1907 (GA 99) and also Note 68.

227. GA 107.

228. In GA 194.

229. Lecture of 15 December 1919 (GA 194).

230. Lecture of 13 January 1924 (GA 233).

231. 'The Laying of the Foundation Stone of the General Anthroposophical Society through Rudolf Steiner, 25 December, 10 o'clock in the Morning' (GA 260).

232. Man's inner overcoming of the three categories of spirits of opposition *by the power of Christ* is at the same time also the beginning of their redemption (see what is said in note 70).

233. Rudolf Steiner speaks in the lecture of 13 June 1915, GA 159/160, about how the 'World Imaginations', drawn by man every night

from the spiritual spheres, become forces of life in his etheric body.

234. The spiritual forces from which the supersensible 'Foundation Stone' was formed by Rudolf Steiner at the Christmas Conference also underlay the 'Foundation Stone Meditation', with the reading of which he began and ended the Christmas Conference (see GA 260). Working with this Meditation has the purpose of deepening and strengthening the spiritual forces that have been referred to. Thus its structure corresponds in every detail to the character of the Foundation Stone. From the standpoint of our present considerations, this means that the first part of the Meditation can help man overcome the Asuras, the second part, Ahriman, and the third Lucifer. However, this can happen only if the Christ Sun shines forth within the human ego. This is spoken of in the fourth part of the Meditation, which enables even the influence of the opposing forces themselves to turn towards the good: 'that good may become'.

235. GA 10, the chapter entitled 'Practical Aspects'.

236. Answer to a question asked after the lecture of 2 September 1906 (GA 95).

237. Lecture of 16 July 1914 (GA 155).

238. See the description of both Guardians of the Threshold in the final chapters of GA 10.

239. In the lecture of 15 June 1924 (GA 239), Rudolf Steiner speaks of how the individuality who was to become Pestalozzi was in his incarnation in the first century AD an overseer of a group of slaves who in the nineteenth century reincarnated as the charges of the great educationalist. Thus Pestalozzi was able through his goodness and care to compensate for the wrong that he had formerly inflicted.

240. Lecture of 2 December 1911 (GA 130).

241. See GA 10, the chapter entitled 'The Conditions of Esoteric Training': the description of the sixth condition.

List of Works by Rudolf Steiner Referred to in the Present Book

The English title is given only in cases where a similar (though not always identical) volume to the original German edition from the collected works—the *Gesamtausgabe* (abbreviated as 'GA')—has been published in English translation. In many cases, lectures are available in typescript or in print as single lectures or compilations from the collected works. For information on these (which are not listed below) contact Rudolf Steiner House Library, 35 Park Road, London NW1 6XT, or similar anthroposophical libraries around the world.

Publishers:

AP:	Anthroposophic Press (New York)
APC:	Anthroposophical Publishing Company (London)
GAR:	Garber Communications, Inc. (New York). Imprint: Spiritual Science Library
MER:	Mercury Press (Spring Valley, New York)
RSP:	Rudolf Steiner Press (London)

GA

4	*The Philosophy of Freedom* (RSP, 1988), or *Intuitive Thinking as a Spiritual Path* (AP, 1995)
9	*Theosophy* (RSP, 1989)
10	*Knowledge of the Higher Worlds* (RSP, 1989), or *How to Know Higher Worlds* (AP, 1994)
11	*Cosmic Memory* (GAR, 1990)
13	*Occult Science* (RSP, 1962)

14   *The Four Mystery Plays* (RSP, 1983)
15   *The Spiritual Guidance of Humanity* (AP, 1992)
26   *Anthroposophical Leading Thoughts* (RSP, 1985)
28   *The Course of My Life* (AP, 1980)
34   *Lucifer-Gnosis*
93   *Die Tempellegende und die Goldene Legende.* Some lectures
          appear in *The Temple Legend* (RSP, 1985)
93a   *Foundations of Esotericism* (RSP, 1983)
95   *At the Gates of Spiritual Science* (RSP, 1970)
96   *Ursprungsimpulse der Geisteswissenschaft*
97   *Das christliche Mysterium*
99   *Theosophy of the Rosicrucian* (RSP, 1981)
102   *The Influence of Spiritual Beings upon Man* (AP, 1961)
103   *The Gospel of St John* (AP, 1984)
104   *The Apocalypse of St John* (RSP, 1985)
107   *Geisteswissenschaftliche Menschenkunde*
109/11   *Das Prinzip der spirituellen Ökonomie im Zusammenhang mit
          Wiederverkörperungsfragen.* Some lectures appear in *The Principle
          of Spiritual Economy* (AP, 1986)
110   *The Spiritual Hierarchies and their Reflection in the Physical World*
          (AP, 1983)
112   *The Gospel of St John and its Relation to the Other Gospels* (AP,
          1982)
113   *The East in the Light of the West* (GAR, 1986)
114   *The Gospel of St Luke* (RSP, 1988)
116   *The Christ Impulse and the Development of Ego Consciousness* (AP,
          1976)
120   *Manifestations of Karma* (RSP, 1984)
123   *The Gospel of St Matthew* (RSP, 1985)
130   *Das esoterische Christentum und die geistige Führung der Mensch-
          heit.* Some lectures appear in *Esoteric Christianity and the Mission
          of Christian Rosenkreutz* (RSP, 1984)
131   *From Jesus to Christ* (RSP, 1991)
132   *The Inner Realities of Evolution* (RSP, 1953)
133   *Earthly and Cosmic Man* (GAR, 1986)
144   *The Mystery of the East and of Christianity* (RSP, 1972)
145   *The Effects of Spiritual Development* (RSP, 1978)
148   *The Fifth Gospel* (RSP, 1995)
151   *Human and Cosmic Thought* (RSP, 1967)
152   *Vorstufen zum Mysterium von Golgotha*